DAVID DAY is the author of *The Tolkien Bestiary* (which has sold over 500,000 copies in twelve languages since its publication in 1979), *Tolkien: The Illustrated Encyclopedia* and *Castles* (also illustrated by Alan Lee). He has always been fascinated by the vast complexities of Tolkien's mythology, particularly in the light of the many posthumously published Tolkien manuscripts. David Day has also published more than twenty other books in the fields of ecology, poetry, natural history, fantasy, mythology and a number of award-winning children's books.

ALAN LEE was born in Middlesex in 1947. He attended the Ealing School of Art, specialising in illustration, and has illustrated a wide range of books, including *Faeries* (with Brian Froud), *The Mabinogion*, *Castles*, *Merlin Dreams* and *Black Ships Before Troy*, the story of *The Iliad*. He is also the creator of the hugely successful and extremely beautiful illustrated edition of *The Lord of the Rings*. He was recently awarded the Kate Greenaway Medal for Children's Book Illustration.

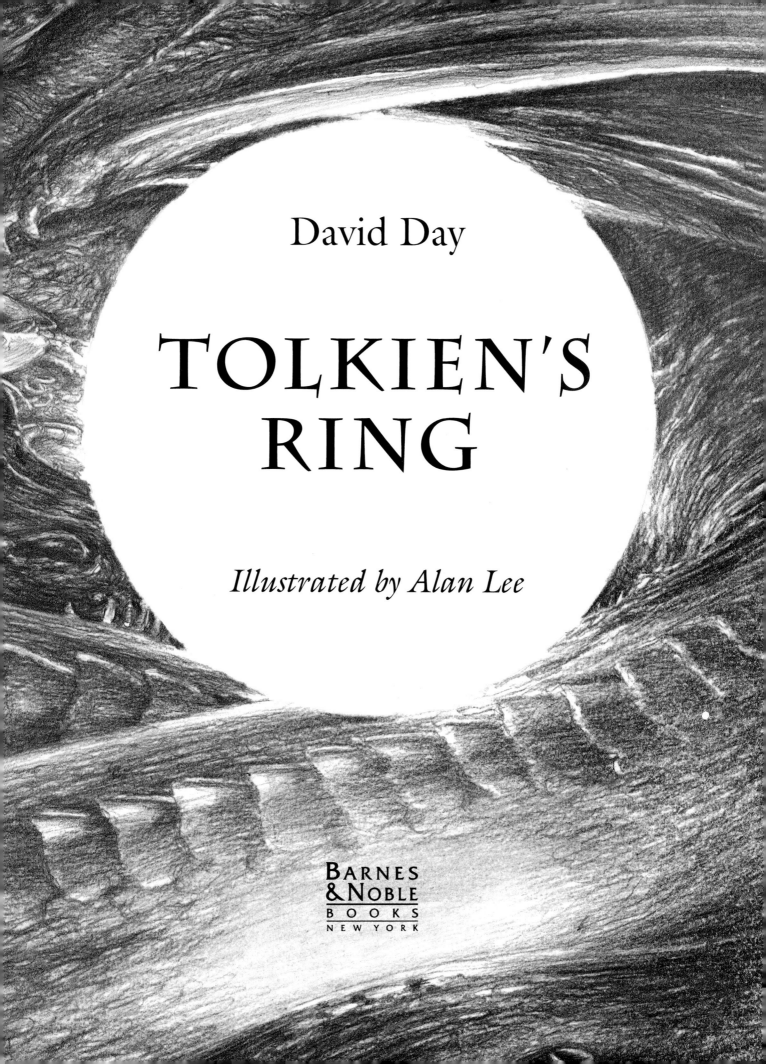

David Day

TOLKIEN'S
RING

Illustrated by Alan Lee

Barnes
& Noble
BOOKS
NEW YORK

This edition published by Barnes & Noble, Inc., by arrangement
with Pavilion Books Limited

1999 Barnes & Noble Books

Text © David Day 1994
Illustrations © Alan Lee 1994

Originally published in 1994 by HarperCollins Publishers

Set in Galliard and Charlemagne

Manufactured in Singapore by Imago

M 10 9 8 7 6 5 4 3 2

ISBN 0-7607-1899-7

To Robin and Sylvia Skelton

CONTENTS

TOLKIEN'S RING

•◆•

CHAPTER ONE

TOLKIEN'S MIND

Tolkien's Ring is a kind of literary detective's casebook that amounts to an investigation of the imagination of J. R. R. Tolkien. In *Tolkien's Ring* we will look into Tolkien's sources of inspiration for his epic fantasy novel, *The Lord of the Rings*. In this investigation, the symbol of the Ring is of primary importance. Through understanding its meaning and significance, we can begin to understand how Tolkien's *The Lord of the Rings* is the result of an ancient story-telling tradition that dates back to the dawn of Western culture.

Tolkien once described how the discovery of the Ring in an Orc cavern by Bilbo Baggins was as much a surprise to the author as it was to his Hobbit hero. Tolkien knew as little of its history as Bilbo Baggins did at that time. He also explained how it grew from a simple vehicle of plot in *The Hobbit* into the central image of his epic tale *The Lord of the Rings*. Just as Tolkien's Wizard Gandalf set out to discover the history of the Hobbit's Ring, so in this book we will search out the history and descent of Tolkien's Ring.

Just how did this Ring come to be so casually discarded in the caverns of Tolkien's mind? The truth is Tolkien's Ring had its origin in a tradition of ring quest tales that came into being before the pyramids of Egypt were built, or the walls of Babylon were raised. While the glorious civilization of Greece and the mighty empire of Rome rose and fell, that tradition lived on. It survived the fall of the pagan gods; and the rise of Buddha, Mohammed and Christ.

Although the ring quest tradition first came into being among tribal peoples long before written records were kept, this does not mean we have no idea of what early forms it took. Remarkably, in the twentieth century, the symbolic rituals of the ring quest remain intact in one of its most elemental forms among the nomadic tribes of Lappland and Siberia. Anthropologists living among the shamanic Lapplanders this century have frequently recorded the ritual enactment of the ring quest.

In this ceremony the shaman or wizard of the tribe places a brass ring on the head of a sacred drum. The designs and markings on the skin of the drum are essentially a cosmic map of human and spirit worlds. The shaman begins to chant and gently tap the rim of the drumhead with his drum hammer, making the ring move and dance. The ring's progress is the journey of the human soul. As the ring moves around the cosmic map, the shaman sings the tale of the soul's perilous journey through the human and spirit worlds.

Tolkien's Ring attempts to link the bookish Oxford don who was J. R. R. Tolkien and that wild tribal shaman to a single tradition spanning more than five thousand years. Tolkien tapping away on his typewriter keys as the wandering soul of his Hobbit hero moves and dances to its pulse is not unlike the shaman tapping his drum. Nor is the journey of Tolkien's Ring across the map of Middle-earth essentially unlike the journey of the shaman's ring across the drum map of his human and spirit worlds.

In his *The Lord of the Rings*, J. R. R. Tolkien awoke something deep in human consciousness through the universal language of mythic images drawn from the early history of mankind. His epic tale made him the heir of an ancient storytelling tradition that used the common symbolic language of myth to create the largest body of invented mythology in the history of literature.

In tracing the sources of Tolkien's Ring, we open to an audience an appreciation of the world of myth and legend from which Tolkien drew his inspiration. The richness of this heritage is evident in his tales and his vast mythological structures. Tolkien was deeply committed to the study of the ancient wisdom of the human soul as preserved in myth and legend.

'I am interested in mythological invention, and the mystery of literary creation,' Tolkien once wrote in a letter to a reader. 'I was from early days grieved by the poverty of my own beloved country: it had no stories of its own, not of the quality that I sought, and found in legends of other lands. There was Greek, and Celtic, and Romance, Germanic, Scandinavian, and Finnish; but nothing English, save impoverished chap-book stuff.'

This was Tolkien's life ambition. So great was this obsession that it could be argued that the undoubted literary merits of Tolkien's epic tale of *The Lord of the Rings* were almost a secondary concern. Important as the novel is, any analysis of Tolkien's life and work makes one aware that his greatest passion and grandest ambition were focused on the creation of an entire mythological system for the English people.

'I had a mind to make a body of more or less connected legend, ranging from the large and cosmogonic, to the level of romantic fairy-story... which I could dedicate simply: to England; to my country.'

The enormity of this undertaking is staggering. It would be as if Homer, before writing the Iliad and the Odyssey, had first to invent the whole of Greek mythology and history. The degree to which he has actually succeeded is remarkable. In large part Tolkien's invented mythology in the popular imagination has definitely become that of England. Furthermore, it is certainly the most complex and detailed invented world in all literature.

The key to Tolkien's world is not so much where it is to be found, but when. 'The theatre of my tale is this earth, the one in which we now live, but the historical period is imaginary,' he wrote. 'The action of the story takes place in North-west of Middle-earth, equivalent in latitude to the coastline of Europe and the north shore of the Mediterranean.'

That imaginary time is a mythical one just before the first human histories, and the rise of any recorded civilization. It begins with the creation of the world known as Arda (Middle-earth and the Undying Lands) within vast spheres of air and light. This world is inhabited by pagan Gods, Elves, Dwarves, Ents, Orcs, Trolls, Dragons – and eventually mortal Men.

We are thirty-seven thousand years into the history of this world before the events related in *The Lord of the Rings* even begin. After the War of the Ring, many millennia pass before leading on 'eventually and inevitably to ordinary history.'

In a footnote to one of his letters, Tolkien estimates our own historic time was some six thousand years after the Third Age, which he suggested put the twentieth century in the Fifth or Sixth Age by Middle-earth's system of reckoning. So, like those who attempt to date the creation of the world back through the texts of the Bible, we may now reckon the time of Tolkien's War of the Ring at something between 4000 and 5000 BC; while the creation of his world of Arda must be placed at 41,000 BC.

Naturally, Tolkien's world of Arda did not come out of nowhere. It was a composite of all Tolkien was: creative author, philologist, historian, folklorist, mythographer, geographer, philosopher, artist. It was once written of Dante: 'Well nigh all the encyclopedic erudition of the Middle Ages was forged and welded, in the white heat of an indomitable will, into the steel-knit structure of the *Divine Comedy*.' Similarly, of Tolkien it can be said that a compression of everything he read, knew, dreamed and believed of Western history and culture went into the creation of his world of Middle-earth and the Undying Lands.

To understand the creative process of Tolkien's mind, it is interesting to look into his essay 'On Fairy-Tales'. Tolkien suggested the process by which fairy tales were traditionally created was well encompassed in the homely metaphor of soup-making: 'Speaking of the history of stories and especially of fairy-stories we may say that the Pot of Soup, the Cauldron of Story, has always been boiling, and to it have continually been added new bits, dainty and undainty.'

Tolkien rather warns us off the task of examining the bones in an attempt to determine the nature of the ox from which the soup is made. 'The history of fairy-stories is probably more complex than the physical history of the human race, and as complex as the history of human language.'

He warns us that 'the intricate web of Story is now beyond all the skill but that of the elves to unravel it.' Certainly, the recipe for Tolkien's Cauldron of Story was very, very complex. Its bones and bits, dainty and undainty, were drawn from a vast range of histories, myths, tales, folklore, sagas. To this was added the magical ingredient of pure invention.

Tolkien's Ring is not an attempt to examine *The Lord of the Rings* page by page, image by image. It will more broadly attempt an investigation into that rich body of literature, myth and history that inspired Tolkien in the creation of his epic novel. These are myths and legends with which Professor Tolkien was intimately acquainted, and about which he often despaired because so few readers in the twentieth century were even vaguely familiar with them.

One of Tolkien's chief vehicles of inspiration for literary invention was philological. He considered himself a philologist above all things. 'I began with language, I found myself involved in inventing legends of the same taste,' he once wrote. It was language itself that suggested a world rather than the other way round.

One of Tolkien's most famous statements came by way of an answer to the question of where Hobbits came from. 'All I remember about the start of *The Hobbit* is sitting correcting School Certificate papers in the everlasting weariness of that annual task forced on impecunious academics with children. On a blank leaf I scrawled, "In a hole in the ground there lived a hobbit." I did not and do not know why.'

After that, it became his task to explain to himself just what a Hobbit was and what it was doing in that hole in the ground. Besides Hobbits, Tolkien created other races and creatures from names he invented himself, like Balrogs, Uruks, and Nazgûl. More typically, however, Tolkien took words from fragments of ancient mythologies and legends. Often he chose Old English words that suggested little or nothing to the average reader. Obscure words like Orc, Ent, Wose were expanded by his inventive mind, and made into striking and original creations. On other occasions, Tolkien took clichés of myth and fairy tale like Elf, Dwarf, Wizard which he vigorously reinvented. To all he gave vibrant life and a vast, newly created world where they might live and breathe.

Central to Tolkien's creative effort was the attempted illusion that Middle-earth was a world of archetypes that survived in the racial unconscious of the English people. All that the English are and know comes from this world. All great events of English history are prefigured in archetypal form in this ancient mythic world.

Throughout his fictional writing, Tolkien employs a favourite literary device of inventing a kind of 'prototype story' which we are encouraged to accept as the 'true event' that would plausibly explain later well-known legends and tales of many nations.

Tolkien's creation and sinking of his mighty island kingdom of Númenor was a deliberate attempt to write the 'true story' behind the myth of Atlantis. In *The Lord of the Rings*, in Prince Aragorn's kiss which awakens the sleeping Princess Éowyn, we are meant to see the 'origin' of the fairy tale of Sleeping Beauty. We are often given prototypes of a species: Glaurung the Golden is the 'Father of Dragons'; Durin the Deathless is one of the 'Seven Fathers of the Dwarves'. Tolkien even gives us a 'true story' behind that well-worn cliché 'Crack of Doom' by turning it into a 'real' and frightening place.

Ultimately Tolkien's Ring itself is intended to be the archetypal Ring on which all other ring quest cycles were based. The truth, of course, is quite the opposite, although Tolkien's Ring makes its unique contribution to that ancient tradition.

This is not to suggest that Tolkien simply plucks figures out of myths and legends. The creative imagination is a complex thing. To demonstrate something of the creative process of Tolkien's mind, we might look at a minor motif unrelated to the ring quest tradition which demonstrates how the raw material is transformed into creative fiction.

Let us take an example of a single source with which most readers will already be familiar: William Shakespeare's *Macbeth*. There can be little doubt that this play was a minor source for certain aspects of Tolkien's novel. Curiously, it was a source of 'negative inspiration'. This was because Tolkien profoundly disliked the play, although he was fascinated with the historic and mythic story of *Macbeth*.

Tolkien appears to have rather enjoyed voicing the ultimate Englishman's heresy of hating Shakespeare altogether. In fact, he went even further and tended to voice his dismissal of drama as a form of literature at all. In his essay 'On Fairy-Stories', Tolkien concluded that drama is essentially hostile to much loved 'fantasy' because it is, in itself, a kind of counterfeit fantasy. Tolkien stated that more than any other form of literature, fantasy needs a 'willing suspension of disbelief' to survive. In dramatized fantasy (like the Witches scene in *Macbeth*) Tolkien found 'disbelief had not so much to be suspended as hanged, drawn and quartered.'

However peculiar Tolkien's dislike of Shakespeare and *Macbeth*, it proved a very fruitful hatred, particularly in relation to the episodes of *The Lord of the Rings* concerning the Ents. Although typically the Ents themselves came from a philological source, the plot element of the mighty 'March of the Ents' was motivated by Shakespeare.

In explaining the origin of his Tree Herds, the Ents, Tolkien wrote: 'I should say that Ents are composed of philology, literature and life. They owe their name to the "*eald enta geweorc*" of Anglo-Saxon.' However, beyond 'Ent' simply being an Anglo-Saxon name for 'giant', the real inspiration was Tolkien's attempt to write the prototype myth behind what he considered a rather limp tale by Shakespeare.

'Their part in the story is due, I think, to my bitter disappointment and disgust from schooldays with the shabby use made in Shakespeare of the coming of "Great Birnam wood to high Dunsinane hill": I longed to devise a setting in which the trees might really march to war.' And so he gives us the 'true story' behind the prophecy in *Macbeth* in the epic March of the Ents on the realm of Saruman of the White Hand.

Tolkien tells us, again in 'On Fairy-Stories': '*Macbeth* is indeed a work by a playwright who ought, at least on this occasion, to have written a story, if he had the skill or patience for that art.' Since Shakespeare was no longer available to take the advice, Tolkien decided to take on the job himself.

In this effort, Tolkien extended himself beyond the marching wood motif. He extended himself by challenging Shakespeare's portrayal of Macbeth himself. Tolkien's evil Lord of the Ringwraiths – the Witch-king of Morgul – who sold his mortal soul to Sauron for a ring of power and the illusion of earthly dominion is meant to suggest to us a grand and ancient archetype for *Macbeth*'s tale of a king possessed of a doomed and blasted soul.

So that none will mistake the comparison, or Tolkien's challenge to Shakespeare, the life of the Witch-king is protected by a prophecy that is almost identical to the final one that safeguards Macbeth. Tolkien's Witch-king 'cannot be slain by the hand of man'; while the similarly deluded Macbeth 'cannot be slain by man of woman born.'

Again, Tolkien's challenge to Shakespeare is largely about what he considers a fairly limp fulfilment of the prophecy. In terms of convincing plot, one must acknowledge that the Witch-king's death by a woman disguised as a warrior with a Hobbit as an accomplice is a much better answer to the fatal riddle than Shakespeare's lawyer's loophole that someone born by caesarean section is not strictly speaking 'of woman born.'

The most important aspect of all this literary fencing is not really whether Tolkien actually succeeded in his challenge to Shakespeare, or anyone else. Nor does it particularly matter whether or not readers of *The Lord of the Rings* register the allusion. The result was that Tolkien's mind was provoked into creating original characters and events that resonate with a depth and power which they inherit from their source.

This was one of the most profound aspects of Tolkien's genius as an author. He combined a natural story-teller's ability and inventiveness with a scholar's capacity to draw from the deep well of myth, legend, literature and history. He breathed life into ancient traditions that, but for him, would have remained forever unknown to millions of modern readers.

In *Tolkien's Ring*, we will survey a vast body of myth and legend in search of Tolkien's sources. We will look at other rings and ring quests, and we will see where many elements of his epic tale were provoked into existence. However, we should never mistake Tolkien's creative process as a mere cobbling together of ancient lore. Richer and more profound though Tolkien's writing is for the ancient tradition it draws on, Tolkien's art is by no means mere imitation. *The Lord of the Rings* is a highly realized and originally conceived novel that has renewed, invigorated and finally reinvented the ring quest for the twentieth century.

●◆●

CHAPTER TWO

WAR OF THE RINGS

In writing his *The Lord of the Rings*, J. R. R. Tolkien did not invent the idea of a sorcerer-king ruling by the supernatural power of a ring. The ancient belief in the power of rings has been with the human race since the dawn of history. So much so that – in Europe in particular – the quest for the ring is the basis of much of its mythology. Furthermore, this belief in supernatural rings did not restrict itself to legends and fairy tales; it is very much a part of history itself.

Even Tolkien's central concept of a 'War of the Ring' has a remarkable historical precedent. The idea that an empire could be ruinously consumed by war because of a ring may appear an unlikely historical event, but Tolkien had no less an authority than the ancient scholar Pliny to inform him that a dispute over a ring was the direct cause of the downfall of the Roman Republic. Pliny wrote that a quarrel over the possession of a ring erupted between the famous demagogue Drusus and the chief senator Caepio. The dispute led directly to a blood feud and the outbreak of the Social Wars, which resulted in the collapse and ruin of the Republic of Rome.

Another historical tradition attributes the downfall of the once mighty sea empire of the Republic of Venice directly to a ring. In its days of glory, Venice was the ruler of the Mediterranean by virtue of its ships. To celebrate its maritime power, the Doge of Venice would sail out into the Adriatic Sea with great pomp and ceremony one day each year. To celebrate Venice's 'marriage' as the 'bride of the sea', the Doge would throw a gold ring into the deep blue waters of the

Adriatic. Several months after one such ceremony, the Doge held a state dinner at which a large fish was served at his table. When the fish was placed on the Doge's plate it was found to have the gold ring in its belly. The return of the wedding-ring was widely interpreted as the sea's rejection of Venice as its bride – and a premonition of disaster for the Republic. Historical events soon confirmed the prophecy. That same year marked the reversal of Venice's fortunes in its battles at sea, and the collapse of the Republic's empire swiftly followed.

Dactyliomancy, or the use of rings for divination and magic, has been seriously practised throughout history. This belief in the power of rings was not a matter of literary invention; it was a part of everyday life. Its practice has been recorded in thousands of instances. It is worth looking at a few remarkable cases in detail.

Holland, 1548

In the year 1548 at Arnhem in what was then Guelderland, one of the city's most respected citizens was brought before the Chancellor accused of sortilege, or enchantment. This man was reputed to be the region's most learned and excellent physician, and knew 'the cure and remedie for all manner of griefs and diseases', according to the churchman-scholar Hegwoad. But his wisdom was not restricted to medicine. He was always 'acquainted with all newes, as well forrein as domesticke.'

Accusers stated that the physician obtained his powers from a ring that he wore on his hand. Witnesses claimed that the doctor – who later became known as the Sorcerer of Courtray – constantly consulted the ring. It was stated that 'the ring had a demon enclosed in it, to whom it behoved him to speak every five days.'

Despite the marked reluctance of the Chancellor to pass judgement on such a valued citizen, he found the evidence was so overwhelming that he had no choice but to find the man guilty. The physician was immediately proscribed for sorcery, and put to death. Curiously, even greater importance was placed on the fate of the ring than the fate of the sorcerer.

The Chancellor commanded that after the execution of the physician, the ring must be cut from his hand. So that all might witness its destruction, the ring was to be taken immediately to the public market. In full view of the citizens of Arnhem, the demon ring was 'to be layd on an anvil and with an iron hammer to be beaten in pieces.'

England, 1376

In the St Albans *Chronicon Anglais* in the year 1376 is recorded the extraordinary trial of Alice Perrers of Anglia, a mistress of Edward, King of England. Alice Perrers was a woman 'neither voluptuous nor beautiful but of smooth tongue' whom Parliament charged with having enchanted the King by use of magic rings.

Through the power of these rings, it was claimed, Alice Perrers had alienated Edward's affections from his queen, involved him in illicit sexual frenzies, and held sway over his judgements in court. In the trial it was revealed that she had a master who was a magician who was found to have effigies of Alice and the King. It was stated that the magician used herbs and incantations devised by the great Egyptian magus Nectanabus, and 'used rings, such as Moses used to make, rings of oblivion and memory so that the King was unable to act any day without consulting his false predictions.'

Because of the King's intervention, it proved impossible to bring down the full and fatal force of the law of the time onto the accused. However, Alice Perrers was banished from the court and noble society forever after.

Byzantium, 370

In the year 370, during the reign of the Roman Emperor Valens, a powerful group of aristocrats feared that their monarch was neither strong enough nor wise enough to remain in power for long. Concerned about their own fate and that of the Empire, the aristocrats secretly consulted an oracle.

The oracle practised dactyliomancy, or 'ring divination'. This form of prophecy was achieved by means of a circle drawn on the temple floor. The circumference of the circle was inscribed with the letters of the alphabet, and a gold ring was suspended from the temple ceiling by a long thread directly over the centre of the circle.

When the question 'Who should succeed to the throne of the Emperor Valens?' was put to the oracle, the gold ring slowly but decisively drifted from letter to letter, and spelled out: 'T-H-E-O-D'.

All who observed the oracle believed this could only mean Theodorus, a man of noble lineage, eminent qualifications and high popularity. However, among the gathering of aristocrats was a spy loyal to Valens. When Valens learned of the oracle, he concluded that Theodorus could only come to power through a conspiracy. Although there was no evidence at all that Theodorus had any intention of plotting against him, the Emperor Valens had the man immediately put to death.

The great British historian Gibbon remarks on the peculiar irony of this well-documented prophecy in his monumental *Decline and Fall of the Roman Empire*. For in the year 378, the wild Visigoth tribes were in open revolt against imperial rule. The barbarian armies had crossed the Danube and threatened to march on the capital itself. The Imperial Army made a valiant and bloody stand at Adrianople but, outnumbered and badly commanded, they were defeated by the Visigoths and the Emperor Valens was killed.

Out of the turmoil that followed conquest, one ruthless general rose to power among the Spanish legions of the west. This man's name was T-H-E-O-D-osius. True to the prophecy of the ring, this unknown warlord seized control of the Empire. He was crowned in Constantinople and became the Emperor Theodosius the Great.

Beyond the vivid testimonies given here, there are thousands of others throughout recorded history that give convincing proof of the widespread belief in the power of rings. In the nineteenth century, Sir Walter Scott wrote in his *Demonology and Witchcraft* that he knew of many cases of individuals who claimed the ability to compel spirits to enter a ring – and from the imprisoned spirit demand answers to questions proposed.

Valid written testimonies were particularly frequent in medieval Europe. In 1431, one of the many serious charges brought against Joan of Arc was that she used magic rings to enchant and cure. Another well-documented medieval case was that of Hieronimus, the Chancellor of Mediolanum, who was brought to ruin and damnation through the false wisdom of a prophetic ring that 'spoke' to him. Still another remarkable case was recorded by a Joaliun of Cambray in 1545. In that case a young child was in thrall to a crystal ring in which he 'could see all that the demons within demanded of him'. The demons of the ring so tormented their slave that in a fit of despair the child smashed the evil crystal ring and broke its spell.

One of the most vivid historic documentations of the belief in the power of the ring occurred in Venice during the fifteenth century. The incident constituted nothing less than a full Faustian battle for a man's soul, rather reminiscent of the numerous struggles Gandalf endured as he watched the One Ring enthral and corrupt others; and even threaten his own soul.

The Venetian case involved a talented artist and sculptor named Pythonickes who was said to possess an enchanted ring. The spirits within this ring seemed full of charm and wisdom, and by its power Pythonickes believed he had gained his reputation as an inspired artist. However, in time, Pythonickes began to fear for his immortal soul and wished to be free of any claim the ring might make on him. Not knowing if he had the strength to rid himself of the ring, he confessed its possession to a preaching friar, whom he knew to be a good and wise man.

Pythonickes begged the friar to listen to the subtle speech of the spirits in the ring, so he might determine whether they be good or evil, but the friar refused outright. The friar commanded that Pythonickes immediately destroy the enchanted ring, but the artist was now so enthralled by the ring that he no longer had the strength of will to do so.

Worse still, as soon as the friar spoke his command, a terrible lamenting cry was said to come from the ring. The evil spirits within offered all manner of wisdom and fame to the friar. Whereupon the friar perceived that soon his own soul would be in jeopardy if he did not act soon. So, in the words of the medieval scholar Mengius, 'The churchman being zealously enraged, with a great hammer broke the ring almost to dust.'

What is going on here? A lot of hysteria about demons and witchcraft? Perhaps, but why does the image of the ring constantly crop up? Most especially, why this idea of talking and prophesying rings?

If we look at the Anglo-Saxon *Exeter Book* – which was compiled and written circa AD 1000 – we find a cryptic statement or unanswered riddle about a ring. It reads: 'I heard of a bright ring interceding well before men, though tongue-less, though it cried not with loud voice in strong words. The precious thing spoke before men, though holding its peace. May men understand the mysterious saying of red gold, the magic speech.'

In part, the *Exeter Book* may be making reference to oracles that used rings long before the coming of Christ. As we saw in the case of the doomed Byzantine Emperor Valens, dactyliomancy was commonly used in the ancient world. The case of Valens' prophecy was, however, only one method of allowing a ring to 'speak'. Another involved water and, as the Latin scholar Peucer described it, would appear to make a quite reasonable lie-detector test: 'A bowl was filled with water, and a ring suspended from the finger was librated in water, and so, according as the question was propounded, a declaration, or confirmation of its truth or otherwise, was obtained. If what was proposed was true, the ring, of its own accord, without any impulse struck the sides of the goblet a certain number of times.'

The ancient Roman Numa Pompilius evidently used this method of divination; while Execetus, the tyrant of the Phocians, used a means of divination based on sounds emitted by the striking of two large rings together. Still other practitioners of dactyliomancy chose to throw rings or stones into pools of water and read the 'rings' as they formed on the still surface. (This particular form of divination is not far removed from that of the prophetic images that appeared in the watery rings of the 'Mirror of Galadriel', which the Elf Queen commanded by the power of her ring, Nenya.)

Curious and entertaining as dactyliomancy may be, however, I do not find it an entirely satisfactory answer to the Exeter riddle about the 'magic speech' of the ring. I do not believe the physician of Arnhem was burned, nor Alice Perrers banished, nor Theodorus impaled for playing 'Ouija' with rings.

What was the answer to the riddle of the 'magic speech' of the ring? Was there a tradition based on the symbol of the ring that runs parallel to the tradition of the symbol of the cross? Is it possible to trace that tradition and understand where and why and how it maintained its force and power through centuries of suppression?

The answer is that the ring was actually the primary symbol of a tradition that the Church saw as being in conflict with orthodox doctrines of Christianity. To understand this one must look at the cult of witchcraft. In Murry's *The Witch Cult in Western Europe*, the author concludes that the so-called 'cult of witchcraft' in one sense was not entirely a figment of the Church's imagination. 'The only explanation of the immense number of witches who were legally tried and put to death in Western Europe is that we are dealing with a religion which was spread over the whole continent and counted its members in every rank of society, from the highest to the lowest.' Murry identifies this 'religion' as the remnant of primitive pagan cults which survive in various states of imperfection throughout Europe.

It is a more than reasonable supposition that aspects of pagan religions survived Christian conversion. In fact, a common tactic in the conversion of pagans was absorption of many aspects of pagan worship into the gospel of the Church. At other times, however, the Christian fathers found that if they had sufficient power it was easier simply to crush any pagan practice that was believed to pose a threat to orthodox Christian doctrines.

If these surviving pagan beliefs were to be represented by any single image in the way that Christianity is represented by the Cross, there is no doubt that that single image was the ring. As we shall see in this book, in Europe the ring was the dominant symbol of all the pagan Teutonic tribes. It was especially the dominant symbol of the Viking warrior culture which was Christian Europe's greatest scourge at the end of the first millennium.

Above all others, the Viking's one-eyed sorcerer god, Odin, was 'the God of the Ring'. (He was Tolkien's primary source of inspiration for his sorcerer 'Sauron, The Lord of the Rings'.) In the same way as the worship of Christ was symbolized by the Cross, the worship of Odin was symbolized by the ring. After the collapse of Roman authority, European Christian settlements, churches and monasteries experienced centuries of relentless Viking terror. It is little wonder that in the simplest terms the Church saw in the symbol of the ring the greatest threat to the authority of the Cross.

It is more complex than this, of course. The ring was a much older symbol of authority than Christianity, and the Church itself adapted its authority in many forms. The Pope wore a ring as the symbol of office; as did all other officers of the Church. Christian marriages were enforced by what amounted to the pagan custom of swearing an oath upon a ring. Nuns were 'wed' to Christ with a gold ring; and in the form of the Celtic Cross, the image of the ring and the Cross were even united as an image suitable for worship in a Christian church.

It was a matter of where a particular ring's power was rooted. In the figure of the early Christianized Viking King Olaf, we see a real blood and thunder missionary who believed he knew where the source of one particular ring's power was to be found. When the Faroe Islands were converted by Olaf, the heroic Faroese chieftain Sigmund Brestesson accepted Christianity as the new faith of his people. However, Olaf learned that Sigmund had kept in his possession one sacred gold ring from the pagan temples. Knowing exactly the symbolic implications of Sigmund's act, King Olaf demanded it be given up to the Church. The milder Christian virtues were not yet apparent in King Olaf. When Sigmund refused to give up the ring, Olaf had him murdered in his sleep.

The ring was also the symbol of the alchemist. The alchemist's ring – in the form of a serpent swallowing its own tail – represented a quest for knowledge that was forbidden by the Church. Alchemists were often executed as sorcerers or magicians. The practices of these alchemists were often linked with their rings. The real or imagined use and trade of such 'rings of power' were perceived as an evil that must be eradicated.

The medieval Frenchman Le Layer, in his curious study *Des Spectres*, wrote about the trade and believed use of such rings:

> With regard to demons whom they imprison in rings, or charms, the magicians of the school of Salamanca and Toledo, and their master Picatrix, together with those in Italy who made traffic of this kind of ware, knew better than to say whether or not they had appeared to those who had them in possession or bought them. And truly I cannot speak without horror of those who pretend such vulgar familiarity with them, even to speaking of the nature of each particular demon shut up in a ring; whether he be a Mercurial, Jovial, Saturnine, Martial, or Aphrodisiac spirit; in what form he is

wont to appear when required; how many times in the night he wakes his possessor; whether benign or cruel in disposition; whether he can be transferred to another; and if, once possessed, he can alter the natural temperament, so as to render men of Saturnine complexion Jovial, or the Jovials Saturnine, and so on.

Because of constant persecution, alchemists cloaked their studies in secrecy and wrote up their experiments and formulae in codified records. The twentieth century's leading historian of religions, Mirca Eliade, concluded that alchemical studies were transmitted mystically, just as poetry uses fables and parables. In alchemy, Eliade wrote: 'What we are dealing with here is a SECRET LANGUAGE such as we meet among shamans and secret societies and among the mystics of the traditional religions.'

This 'secret language' is strongly reminiscent of the *Exeter Book*'s 'magic speech' of the ring. It seems likely that we are dealing with the same kind of cryptic communication. The 'magic speech' of the ring and the 'secret language' of alchemy are one. The dominance of the symbol of the ring in pagan religions – and in all shamanistic tribal cultures who use metal – is related to the ring's alchemical origins.

The secret of the ring is in its making. To make a ring, one must have the knowledge to smelt and forge metal. The 'secret language' of the alchemist symbolized by the ring was his knowledge of metallurgy. Ultimately, this is concerned with the secret of the smelting and forging of iron, which is believed to have been discovered around 1000 BC in the region of the Caucasian Mountains. It was the atomic secret of its day, a secret that was closely guarded: where the ore was mined, how the metal was extracted, how it was forged into weapons and tools.

Those who possessed the secret conquered and often exterminated those who did not. The Iron Age transformed nations of timid shepherds and farmers into ferocious warriors capable of catastrophic feats of destruction on their once powerful, and now subjugated, neighbours. The hero who won the alchemist's 'ring' in the form of the secret of iron-smelting literally saved his nation.

The arts of the smith and the occult

sciences are overlapping techniques handed down as trade secrets with their own rites and rituals. The mysteries of initiation rites and the secret language of the rituals of the trade became symbols in mythic tales.

Robert Graves, the poet and scholar of myth, gives us an excellent example of decoding the 'secret language' of myth in his analysis of the Cyclopses, those one-eyed giants of Greek mythology. The Cyclopses were the counterparts of the Teutonic Dwarfs. Like the Dwarfs (and even Tolkien's Dwarves) they were a race of smiths who lived beneath the mountains and forged wondrous weapons.

> Cyclopses seem to have been a guild of early helladic bronze-smiths. Cyclops means 'ring-eyed' (not 'one-eyed') and they are likely to have been tattooed with concentric rings on their forehead, just as the Thracians continued to tattoo themselves until classical times. Concentric rings are part of the mysteries of smith-craft... The Cyclopses were one-eyed also in the sense that smiths often shade one eye with a patch against flying sparks. Later, their identity was forgotten and became fanciful.

Many scholars, from J. G. Frazer in *The Golden Bough* to Jessie Weston in *From Ritual to Romance*, have demonstrated how the rituals and rites of fertility cults connected with agriculture have manifested themselves in the language of mythology. What is less commonly recognized is the profound impact the rituals and rites of metallurgy have had on myth.

However, it is not so much the techniques of metallurgy that are conveyed in these myths, but the secret rituals of initiation into those cults and the spiritual rites practised within the guild which evolve into the symbols of myth. The symbolic language of the ring quest, at its most profound, is concerned with the 'spiritual' consequences of the Bronze and Iron Ages which changed forever the human condition and perception of the world.

Mirca Eliade emphasizes this point: 'Before changing the face of the world the Iron Age engendered a large number of rites, myths and symbols which have reverberated throughout the spiritual history of humanity.'

If one looks at the ring quest myths of most cultures, there are certain constants for the hero in his pursuit of the ring: the magician, the smith, the warrior, the sword, the dwarf, the maiden, the treasure, and the dragon. These all relate originally to the rites and processes of metallurgy, and later to the symbolic 'secret language' of the alchemist's ring.

In the *Lord of the Rings* we have all the elements of the ring quest, and yet something wholly original in his own War of the Ring.

CHAPTER THREE

NORSE MYTHOLOGY

No people in history were as obsessed with the power of the ring as the Vikings. The ring was wealth, honour, fame and destiny to these warrior people. Under its sign they charted unknown seas, waged barbarous wars, sacrificed man and beast, pledged their faith, made great gifts of it, and finally died for it. Their gods were ring lords of the heavens, and their kings were ring lords of the earth.

The longship's figurehead was a ring: clenched in a dragon's teeth or carved itself with the scales of the worm. It broached the grey horizons of the North Sea and Dublin Bay, pointed the way to Spain, Italy, Tangier and Byzantium across the blue Mediterranean, and swept through the icy seas of the North Atlantic and the fog-banks of America. The ring-prowed ships heralded fire, death and destruction.

No earthly king or earl who was not a 'ring-giver' held power long. For by these gifts of wealth and honour, the warrior expected his reward for his faithfulness. From looted gold, the king's smith would fashion heavy engraved finger rings, massive arm rings and great neck rings of woven gold. These were all symbols of nobility, wealth and fame. Thus, often a kingdom's power might rightly be judged by the 'ring-hoard' of the king.

In the ring quest myths of the Vikings, that ferocious warrior culture of Norsemen, we see one of the primary sources of inspiration for Tolkien's fantasy epic, *The Lord of the Rings*. Although the symbol of the ring was widespread and prominent in many far more ancient cultures, it was the Norsemen who brought the ring quest to its fullest expression, and to the very heart of their cultural identity. Virtually all subsequent ring quest tales in myth and fiction are deeply indebted to the Norse myths. Tolkien's *The Lord of the Rings*, although striking in its originality and innovation, is no exception.

Among the Vikings, the gold ring was a form of currency, a gift of honour, and sometimes an heirloom of heroes and kings. (Such a ring belongs to the Swedish Royal House, the Swedish kings' ring known as Sviagriss.) Other times, when great heroes or kings fell, and it was thought none other would be worthy of the honour of the ring lord, the ring-hoard was buried with its master.

So, in barrow and cave, in mere and grave, upon burial ship sunk beneath the sea, the rings slept with their ring lords. Afterward tales were told of dead men's curses and supernatural guardians. In Norse myth and in Tolkien's tales, guardians of treasures and ring-hoards take many forms: damned spirits, serpents, dragons, giants, dwarfs, barrow-wights, and demon monsters.

The rings of Norse mythology – like Tolkien's – were commonly magical rings forged by Elves. These gold rings were tokens of both power and eternal fame. They were also symbolic of the highest power: destiny, the cycle of doom.

Indeed, the Domhring, the Ring of Doom – the ring of monolithic stones that stood before the Temple of Thor – was perhaps the most dreaded symbol of the violent law of the Vikings. (In Tolkien, an identically named 'Ring of Doom' stands outside the gates of Valimar, the city of the gods.) In the centre of this ring of stones was the Thunder God's pillar, the Thorstein. The histories tell us of its use. In the ninth century the Irish King Maelgula Mac Dungail was made captive in the Viking enclave of Dublin. He was taken to the Ring of Doom and his back was broken upon Thorstein. Of another such ring in Iceland a scribe in the Christian twelfth century wrote that bloodstains could still be seen upon the central stone.

Yet the great pillared temple of the fierce, red-bearded Thunder God housed another very different – but to Norse society infinitely more important – ring. Thor's weapon was the thunderbolt, the Hammer called Mjolnir 'the Destroyer', but Thor's most valued gift to mankind was the altar ring that was housed in his temple. This was the Oath Ring of Thor, the emblem of good faith and fair dealing.

On the sacred altar was a silver bowl, an anointing twig, and the Oath Ring itself. Whether of gold or silver, it must weigh more than twenty ounces. Thor's statue, mounted in his goat-drawn chariot, dominated the sanctuary while around the altar were grouped the twelve figures of his fellow gods, their eyes fixed upon the ring.

When an oath was to be taken, an ox was brought in and slaughtered and the *hlaut*, the sacred blood, was sprinkled on the ring. Then the man laid his hand upon the ring and, with Thor gazing down on him, faced the people and said aloud: 'I am swearing an oath upon the Ring, a sacred oath; so help me Freyr, and Njorthr and Thor the Almighty ...'

For the Vikings such an oath was legally binding, and when the world's first democratic parliament, the Althing, was established in Iceland in AD 930 the temple priests brought out the Oath Rings to reinforce its law.

Yet Thor was not the only ring lord among the gods, nor was the power of his ring supreme. The greatest power was in the ring on the hand of Odin, the Magician-King of the gods. Odin was the Allfather, Lord of Victories, Wisdom, Poetry, Love and Sorcery. He was Master of the Nine Worlds of the Norse universe, and through the magical power of his ring was, quite literally, 'the Lord of the Rings'.

But Odin was not always almighty and his quests for power and his magical ring were long and were achieved at great cost. He travelled throughout the Nine Worlds on his quests and hid himself in many forms, but most often he appeared as an old man: a bearded wanderer with one eye. He wore a grey or blue cloak and a traveller's broad-brimmed slouch hat. He carried only a staff and was the model for the wandering Wizard and Magicians from Merlin to Gandalf.

However, before going further into the myth of Odin's ring, it is worthwhile and necessary to take a broad overview of Tolkien's Middle-earth and compare it to the lands of Norse mythology. Although Tolkien's world is profoundly different in many of its basic moral and philosophical perspectives from that of Viking mythology, similarities are numerous and significant.

The most immediate parallel for anyone even mildly familiar with Norse myth is that the world of mortal men in both have the same name: the Norse 'Midgard' literally translates to 'Middle-earth'.

The immortal gods of the Norsemen are made up of two races: the Aesir and the Vanir; while Tolkien's gods are originally called the Ainur, but become known as the Valar in their earthly form. In both systems, the gods live in great halls or palaces in a world apart from mortal lands. The Aesir live in Asgard which can only be reached by crossing the Rainbow Bridge on the flying horses of the Valkyries. Tolkien's Valar live in Aman which can only be reached by crossing the 'Straight Road' in the flying ships of the Elves.

Norse cosmology was rather more complex than Tolkien's in its elemental structure. Asgard and Midgard were just two of its nine 'worlds'. However, Tolkien's 'worlds' are far more cosmopolitan and most of the inhabitants of the nine Norse worlds are recognizable within his two.

31

Besides the worlds of Midgard and Asgard, Norse myths tell of the worlds called Alfheim and Swartalfheim: the realms of the Light Elves and the Dark Elves. These were parallel to Tolkien's Elves who are divided into two great races: the Eldar who are (for the most part) Light Elves, and the Avari who are Dark Elves.

The Dwarfs of Viking mythology were also given their own world. This was a dark underground world of caves and caverns called Nidavellir which was found beneath Midgard, where the Dwarfs constantly worked their mines. These Dwarfs share many of the characteristics of Tolkien's Dwarves, although in Tolkien both Dwarves and Elves are more highly defined and individual, and their genealogies are far more complex.

It is notable that Tolkien took the names of most of his Dwarves directly from the text of Iceland's twelfth-century *Prose Edda*. The *Edda* gives an account of the creation of the Dwarfs, then lists their names. All the Dwarves in the Hobbit appear on this list: Thorin, Dwalin, Balin, Kíli, Fíli, Bifur, Bofur, Bombur, Dori, Nori, Ori, Óin and Glóin. Others names of Dwarfs which Tolkien found in the *Prose Edda* included Thráin, Thrór, Dáin and Nain. The *Edda* also gives the name Durin to a mysterious creator of the Dwarfs which Tolkien uses for his first Dwarf king of 'Durin's Line'. Rather surprisingly, another of the Icelandic Dwarfs is called Gandalf. Undoubtedly, it was the literal meaning of Gandalf – 'sorcerer elf' – that appealed to Tolkien when choosing this name for his wizard.

The Norsemen gave two worlds to their races of Giants: Jotenheim and Muspellsheim. Jotenheim was the home of the cave-dwelling Rock and Frost Giants. In them we see the recognizable characteristics of the large, stupid and easily outwitted monsters that evolved into the Trolls of Scandinavian fairy tales. In Tolkien, these became his similarly stupid Stone Trolls and Snow Trolls.

In the world of Muspellsheim, however, we find the far more formidable Fire Giants. Undoubtedly Fire Giants are personifications of volcanic subterranean powers. For once released from Muspellsheim, Fire Giants were virtually unstoppable. In Ragnarok, the final battle of gods and giants at the end of time, they played a major part in the destruction of the world. In Tolkien we see something of these terrible titans in his creation of the Balrogs, the fiery 'demons of might'.

Another world was Vanaheim, the home of the second race of gods, the Vanir – a race of nature spirits of the earth and air who are also magicians capable of casting terrifying spells. In Norse myth these magician gods are not clearly defined like dominant Aesir gods, but they seem to resemble Tolkien's Valar in their early manifestations as elemental spirits or 'forces of nature'.

The deepest world of all was Niflheim, the dark and misty land of the dead. In this cold and poisoned land was the great walled citadel of Hel, the goddess of the dead. The gate of the fortress of Hel was guarded by Garm the Hound, and within were imprisoned the damned spirits of the dead. This is comparable in Tolkien's *Silmarillion* to the cold and poisoned land of Angband ('iron-fortress') which is ruled by Morgoth, the god of darkness. The gate of the fortress of Angband was guarded by Carcharoth the Wolf and within were imprisoned many Elves who were hideously tortured and transformed into a race of damned beings called Orcs. By the time of the War of the Rings, Morgoth's disciple Sauron attempts to recreate Angband in his dark and evil Land of Mordor.

Ultimately, Norse myth and Tolkien's fiction both had cosmologies that share a stoic fatalism in their ultimate destiny. In Viking myth, the spirits of slain warriors are gathered in the Hall of Valhalla in Asgard: while in Tolkien's tales, the spirits of slain Elves inhabit the Halls of Mandos in Aman. Both remain there and await the time when they are called to participate in the cataclysms that will end their worlds. This is the great conflict of elemental forces that the Vikings called Ragnarok and Tolkien called the World's End.

Tolkien's vision of his World's End is deliberately veiled, but we see some comparisons between the Viking Ragnarok – when the rebel god Loki led the Giants into battle against the gods – and Tolkien's cataclysmic Great Battle in *The Silmarillion*. When Eönwë the Herald of the Valar blew his trumpet, the Valar went into battle against the rebel Vala Morgoth and his monstrous servants at the end of the First Age of Sun. The Viking Ragnarok was a battle between the gods and the Giants which similarly commenced when Heimdall the Herald of the Gods blew his horn. Ragnarok ended with the destruction of all the Nine Worlds. Tolkien's Great Battle resulted in the total destruction of Morgoth and his evil kingdom of Angband, but it also tragically caused the beautiful Elvish realms of Beleriand to sink beneath the sea.

Some tales in Tolkien's writing directly echo episodes in that cataclysm of Ragnarok. In the Quest of the Silmaril, the hero Beren attempts to use the fiery Silmaril to drive back Carcharoth the Giant Wolf of Angband. However, the beast bites off Beren's hand at the wrist and swallows both hand and the flaming jewel. Carcharoth the Red Maw is filled with horrific pain as the jewel sears his accursed flesh and consumes his evil soul from within. The great beast is like a raging meteor loose in the land, full of pain and wrathful power until at last he is slain.

In Tolkien's tale, Carcharoth is comparable to the Norse myth of Fenrir the Giant Wolf who bit off the hand of Tyr, the heroic son of Odin. Fenrir was the

monstrous offspring of the evil rebel god Loki, and like Carcharoth was the largest and most powerful Wolf in the spheres of the world. During Ragnarok, the Wolf devoured the sun which burned and consumed him from within, but filled him with wrathful power until at last he was slain.

In *The Lord of the Rings*, Gandalf's battle with the Balrog of Moria mirrors another duel in Ragnarok. In the giant Balrog of Moria who fights the Wizard Gandalf with a sword of flame on the stone bridge of Khazad-dûm we have a diminished version of Surt the Fire Giant who fights the god Freyr with a sword of flame on the Rainbow Bridge of Bifrost. Both duels end in disaster when the bridges collapse beneath them and all the combatants hurtle down in a rage of flame.

Although both Tolkien and the Norsemen share a cataclysmic vision of the end of their cosmologies, this vision is not without hope. Out of these conflicts, both promise that this ending is also a transition: a newer, better and more peaceful world is to be reborn from the violent old one.

Tolkien's inspiration is drawn from a far wider range of sources than this brief comparison of cosmologies suggests. However, the influence of Norse myth in the shaping of Tolkien's world is undeniable. This becomes even more evident when we examine ring myths of that civilization; and especially those myths that relate to the king of the Viking gods, Odin.

CHAPTER FOUR

THE GOD OF THE RING

Odin was the supreme god of the Viking culture. He was a god, poet, sorcerer, warrior, trickster, transformer, necromancer, mystic, shaman, and king. Odin is also the single most important figure in any nation's mythology as a source of inspiration for Tolkien in his creation of *The Lord of the Rings*. In Odin's character we can see *both* of Tolkien's great magicians: Gandalf the Grey, and Sauron the Ring Lord.

In Odin we find one of the most complex and ambivalent figures in mythology. He is like a force of nature that is totally uninhibited by moral notions of good and evil. In his actions and deeds, he is not concerned with the morals of humans, but with the acquisition and use of power.

This is a fundamental difference between the Norse Midgard and Tolkien's Middle-earth. The Norse mythic world is essentially amoral, while Tolkien's world is consumed by the great struggle between the forces of good and evil. Consequently, the attributes of the Norse world's greatest Wizard, Odin, are necessarily split in two in Tolkien's morality tale: the 'good' aspects of Odin are found in the Wizard Gandalf, and the 'bad' aspects are found in the Wizard Sauron.

The entire epic tale of *The Lord of the Rings* is primarily about the struggle for control of the world by these conflicting powers as embodied in this duel between the white Wizard and the black Wizard. And Tolkien's single great message – entirely inexplicable to the philosophy and aspirations of the Norsemen – is that 'power corrupts'.

Tolkien's ring quest tale is about the corruption implicit in a quest for pure power, and how the pursuit of power is in itself evil. We soon learn that even when that power (as embodied in the ultimate power of the One Ring) is pursued for reasons that appear essentially 'good', it will necessarily corrupt the quester. We see this in Saruman who was originally a 'good' Wizard who demonstrated the classic moral error of believing 'the end justifies the means'. In his attempt to overthrow the forces of the 'evil' Sauron, Saruman gathers forces that in themselves are just as evil, and is himself corrupted by this desire for power. Unwittingly, Saruman becomes a mirror image and ally of the evil being he initially wished to overcome.

In the 'good' Wizard Gandalf, we see his wisdom and strength of will in his refusal to take possession of the One Ring for a single moment, for fear of his own corruption. He knows full well that he would be morally destroyed by it as surely as was Saruman.

In the myths of the Norsemen, all these particular dilemmas did not exist. These morally conflicting aspects are all embodied in the single figure of Odin the Wizard in his quest for dominion over the Nine Worlds. We see the lonely figure of Odin the Traveller who had nothing but his wits to acquire the power he desired. In his wandering years, we see that his life ultimately was a ring quest for his own 'One Ring'. This was the magical ring called 'Draupnir' whose acquisition was a proclamation to all that Odin had become the 'Ring Lord of the Nine Worlds'.

Although the worlds of the Norsemen were not complicated by Tolkien's moral scruples, they were nevertheless aware that such quests exacted a price. Odin the wanderer was a seeker of knowledge and visions. He travelled the Nine Worlds asking questions of every living thing: Giants, Elves, Dwarfs, Nymphs, and spirits of the air, water, earth and woods. He questioned the trees, plants and the very stones themselves. Odin often endured many trials and dangerous adventures, but from each he wrung what wisdom there was from all things he encountered.

As Odin wandered unnoticed about Midgard – in much the manner as Tolkien's 'Istari' Wizards (who in origin were of the Valarian race of 'gods') wandered Middle-earth – his wisdom and power increased.

Like Radagast the Brown, Odin learned the languages of the birds and beasts. Like Saruman the White, he acquired the honeyed tongue of poets and orators. Like Sauron the Ring Lord, he acquired mastery over wolves and ravens (or crows in Sauron's case). Like Gandalf the Grey, Odin acquired a magical horse which outruns the storming winds.

It has often been observed that nearly all religions have arisen out of the 'supernatural' traditions of shamanism, a set of beliefs common to virtually all tribal peoples, and known to have been practised since the very dawn of human culture. The shaman is a magician, mystic, healer and poet. He travels between the worlds of men and the worlds of spirits and animals, and even to the land of the dead. He makes his ascent or descent by going into a trance. In this state his spirit self may become a bird (often a raven), or it may ride on the back of an animal (often a magical horse), or it may simply take his own human form. But in whatever form, the shaman's spirit self most often reaches the 'other worlds' by climbing a 'cosmic tree' which pierces the heart of the various spirit worlds.

In Norse myth, we have 'Yggdrasil', the great ash tree, whose mighty limbs support the Nine Worlds. Yggdrasil's top is in the heavens above Asgard, and its roots are beneath Hel. Beyond its purpose as a pillar to support these worlds, Yggdrasil is the means by which the journey between these worlds may be made.

Thus, we seem to have the reason for the name 'Yggdrasil', which literally means 'the steed of Ygg [Odin]'. In many respects Odin is the 'supreme shaman'. For just as the shaman climbs or rides up his tree in his trance, so Odin rides Yggdrasil to the Nine Worlds.

It was on Yggdrasil that Odin underwent his most harrowing rites of passage. Like the crucified Christ, Odin was wounded by a spear and hung from the sacred tree for nine days and nine nights. Hanging from the tree in great pain, Odin maintained a state of meditation on the markings cut in the stone by Yggdrasil's roots. By the ninth night Odin deciphered the marking and discovered the secret of the magical alphabet known as 'runes'.

By the power of the runes his own resurrection was achieved. From Yggdrasil he cut the limb he was hung from and made his magician's staff. By the magic of runes Odin could cure, make the dead speak, render weapons powerless, gain women's love, and calm storms by land and sea.

Then ever thirsting for more knowledge, Odin went to drink from the Fountain of Wisdom at the Yggdrasil's foot – and for this too there was a price. For one deep draught from the fountain, Odin must sacrifice an eye. Without hesitation, he drank and from that time he was always the one-eyed god.

In *The Lord of the Rings*, we see something of Odin's rites of passage in Gandalf the Grey's seemingly fatal battle with the Balrog. This conflict and a subsequent mystic inner journey, not unlike Odin's, eventually results in the resurrection of a supercharged Gandalf the White. Gandalf, who already knew how to read runes, rapidly demonstrates many new powers, the least being the ability to render weapons powerless.

With the evil Sauron, we see a Wizard insanely obsessed with the acquisition

of power. Odin becomes the one-eyed lord because he sacrifices the other eye in his quest. Sauron becomes the one-eyed lord because he sacrifices *everything* but that one evil eye. Nothing remains of his spirit and soul but that one fiery evil eye.

In Norse myth, this last inward journey of Odin on Yggdrasil was his making as the Magician-King. Odin ascended to Asgard where the other gods saw his might and wisdom, and all acknowledged them. Similarly, in Tolkien, all the 'Free Peoples' of Middle-earth recognized the might and wisdom of the resurrected Gandalf; and the forces of darkness recognized and accepted the dominion of Sauron in his final resurrection as the 'Eye'.

In his resurrected form, Odin was a fearful god to look on. He was stern, one-eyed, grey-bearded and of gigantic size. He wore a grey cloak with a broad blue mantle and a warrior's eagle-winged helmet. At his feet crouched the two fierce wolves of war ('Ravener' and 'Greed') and on one shoulder perched his two raven messenger-spies ('Thought' and 'Memory'). Tolkien's king of gods, Manwë the Lord of the Air, is rather more in the style of the Olympian Zeus; however, he does share some of Odin's characteristics. He is stern, grey-bearded, of gigantic size, and wears a blue-mantled cloak. He is also the god of poetry, and the wisest and most powerful of gods.

As the King of the Gods, Odin possessed three great halls in Asgard. The first was Valaskiaff where he sat on his golden throne called Hlidskialf, the watch-tower of the gods. From here Odin's one eye could see all that happened in all the Nine Worlds.

In Tolkien's world there are three variations on Odin's throne. Manwë, the King of the Valar, is enthroned on Taniquetil, the highest mountain in the world, and his all-seeing eyes can see over all the world. Sauron's One Eye has similar, if somewhat more limited, power in its ability to see and command his domain from the Dark Tower of Mordor. And Frodo Baggins, the Hobbit, discovers the 'Seat of Seeing' on Amon Hen, 'the hill of the eye'. Once he sits on its stone throne, like a little Odin, he can see telescopically for hundreds of miles in all directions.

Odin's second hall was called Gladsheim. This was the Council Hall of the Gods where Odin presided over the throne ring of the twelve other gods. This is comparable to the Ring of Doom, or Council of the Valar, presided over by Manwë, at the gates of Valimar in the Undying Lands of Aman.

Most famous of all of Odin's halls was Valhalla, the 'hall of the slain', the golden hall of warriors. This is the great feasting-hall with 540 doors and a roof fashioned from shields of polished gold, presided over by Odin, Lord of Victories. Here warriors who fall in battle are rewarded for their bravery by unending feasting and drinking. And there they remain until the time of Ragnarok. In Tolkien we have the rather more gloomy Hall of Awaiting in the Mansions of Mandos the Speaker of Doom in the Undying Lands. However, in common with the Viking warriors, the spirits of slain Elves await the call for the final cataclysm of the World's End.

As emblems of office, Odin was presented with two great gifts. Odin's magician's staff was taken to Alfheim where the Elf-smith Dwalin forged the head of the spear, Gungnir, the most fearful weapon of the Lord of Victories. In Tolkien an echo of this weapon is seen in the magical spear 'Aeglos', the most dreaded weapon of Gil-galad, the last High King of the Elves of Middle-earth.

However, the supreme gift, and the ultimate manifestation of the wealth and power of the Magician-King, was the ring called 'Draupnir'. In Tolkien's tale, all the skill of the Elf Celebrimbor, the most wondrous smith of Middle-earth, and all the wisdom of Sauron went into the forging of the Rings of Power. In Norse myth all the skill of the Elfs Sindri and Brok, the greatest smiths in the Nine Worlds, and all the wisdom of Odin were invested in the forging of the ring 'Draupnir'.

'Draupnir' means 'the dripper', for this magical golden ring had the power to drip eight other rings of equal size every nine days. Its possession by Odin was not only emblematic of his dominion of the Nine Worlds but consolidated his accumulated powers by giving him a source of almost infinite wealth. In his capacity as the King of the Gods, Draupnir gave him the greatest ring-hoard and allowed him to become the greatest ring-giver in the Nine Worlds.

With the acquisition of Draupnir, Odin's quest for dominion was completed. It can be no accident that Draupnir spawns eight other rings of equal weight in nine days. Through Draupnir, Odin rules Asgard, while the other eight are used by Odin the Ring Lord as gifts of wealth and power by which the other eight worlds are governed. Like the earthly Viking king who as a 'ring-giver' rewards his earls, so Odin maintains the order of the other eight worlds by his gift of rings to chosen heroes and kings. The ring on his hand is the ultimate source of all magical rings and all wealth. Through his control of Draupnir, Odin literally becomes the 'Lord of the Rings'.

Among the many legends of Odin, one above all others deals with the ring Draupnir. This is the legend concerning the death of Odin's favourite son, Balder. After the slaying of Balder, he was placed in the huge funeral ship called Ringhorn and all the gods gathered to pay homage. Each laid a gift of unspeakable wonder in his ship. However, so great was Odin's grief that in a frenzy of despair he placed Draupnir on his son's breast just as the ship was set alight and entirely consumed in flames.

This was a tragic error, for without the ring Odin's mastery of the Nine Worlds was in danger of being challenged by the Giants. The ring was needed to restore order to the Nine Worlds. Fortunately, the ring did not perish in the funeral flames, but went with the spirit of Balder into the dark realm of Hel, the prison of the dead.

So a journey must be made down the 'cosmic tree' to recover the ring. To achieve this quest, Odin mounts his magical eight-legged steed Sleipnir and rides down into the deepest realm of Hel. Once there, Sleipnir leaps over the chained Hound of Hel and the great gate it guards as well. Both rider and steed enter into the domain of the damned, seize the sacred ring and ride back. Once Draupnir is restored to Odin in Asgard, peace and order are restored to the Nine Worlds.

In Tolkien's *The Lord of the Rings* we have exactly the opposite scenario in Sauron the Ring Lord's evil quest to recover his One Ring. Sauron is master of a domain of the damned – the hell-on-earth called Mordor – when the One Ring is taken from him. The Ring should then have been consumed by the flames of Mount Doom, but instead it is taken out of the kingdom of the damned into the mortal world where it is lost. Once Sauron returns to Mordor, he sends his Dark Riders into the living world in an attempt to recover the One Ring. It is obvious that if his ring quest is achieved and the One Ring is restored to Sauron in Mordor, the result will be exactly the opposite of Odin's tale. Chaos and war would certainly consume and destroy all of the world.

CHAPTER FIVE

•◆•

THE VOLSUNGA SAGA

The most famous ring legend of the Norsemen is told in the 'Volsunga Saga'. The epic tale is one of the greatest literary works to survive the Viking civilization. Within the 'Volsunga Saga' is the history of many of the heroes of the Volsung and Nibelung* dynasties. In the nineteenth century William Morris wrote of the epic: 'This is the great story of the North, which should be to all our race what the tale of Troy was to the Greeks.'

The fates of the Volsung and Nibelung dynasties were bound up with that of a magical ring called 'Andvarinaut'. This was the magical ring that once belonged to Andvari the Dwarf. It seems to have been an earthly Draupnir. Its name means 'Andvari's loom' because it 'wove' its owner a fortune in gold; and with that wealth went power and fame. The tale of Andvarinaut has become the archetypal ring legend, and is primarily concerned with the life and death of the greatest of all Norse heroes, Sigurd the Dragonslayer.

It is this legend of Sigurd and the Ring as told in the Volsunga Saga that in various forms survives in the modern imagination as 'the' ring legend. William Morris brought the first satisfactory direct translation of the Volsunga Saga into the English language. His later long epic poem 'Sigurd the Volsung', Henrik

---

*In earliest recorded sagas, the Nibelungs were called the Guikings. However, the names appear to be used interchangeably. Iceland's Snorri Sturluson, in the thirteenth-century *Younger Edda*, states: 'Gunnar and Hogni were called Nibelungen or Guikings; therefore the gold is called the Nibelungen hoard.' To minimize the confusion in view of later Germanic traditions, I will use the Nibelung name for the dynasty.

Ibsen's play *The Vikings of Helgeland*, and – above all – Richard Wagner's great opera cycle *The Ring of the Nibelung* brought the epic tale into the popular European imagination in the nineteenth and twentieth centuries.

In this chapter, the Volsunga Saga is retold. It should be noted that the epic is a collection of over forty linked but individual saga tales. These were the final outcome of an oral tradition of diverse authorship composed over many centuries. The resulting texts therefore often result in a somewhat irregular plot structure, although the overall outline is clear. In this retelling, those parts of the saga concerning the ring are emphasized in detail, while peripheral adventures (particularly those that precede the appearance of Sigurd) are told in synopsis form.

Readers will find many parallels between the Volsunga Saga and Tolkien's *The Lord of the Rings* and *The Silmarillion*. Rather than break up the tale with interjections, these parallels will be examined later, along with comparisons with the legends of King Arthur, Charlemagne, Dietrich von Berne, and numerous other heroes and traditions; including the medieval German Nibelungenlied and a score of fairy tales.

The Volsunga Saga begins with the tale of the hero Sigi who is the mortal son of Odin. He is a great warrior who by his strength and skill becomes the King of the Huns. King Sigi's son is Reric, who is also a mighty warrior, but cannot give his queen a child and heir. So the gods send to Reric a crow with an apple in its beak. Reric gives this apple to his wife who eats it and becomes heavy with child. But the child remains in his mother's womb for six years before he is released by the midwife's knife. This child is Volsung, who becomes the third in this line of kings.

Volsung is the strongest and most powerful of all the kings of Hunland. He is a man of huge physical size and he sires ten sons and one daughter. The eldest of his children are the twin brother and sister, Sigmund and Signy.

One day a grey-bearded stranger with one eye appears in the great hall of the Volsungs in the midst of a great gathering of Huns, Goths and Vikings. Without a word, the old man strides over to Branstock, the great living oak tree that stands in the centre of the Volsungs' hall. He draws a brilliant sword from a sheath and drives it up to its hilt in the tree trunk. The ancient stranger then walks out of the hall and disappears.

No mortal man could have achieved such a feat, and all know that this old man can be none other than Odin. All the heroes in the great hall desire this sword, but only Sigmund has the strength to draw it from Branstock. All know that, armed with Odin's sword, Sigmund is the god's chosen warrior.

With this sword, which can cut stone and steel, Sigmund wins great fame, yet terrible tragedy soon befalls the Volsung family. Sigmund's sister is married to the King of Gothland who treacherously murders King Volsung at the wedding feast. He then imprisons Volsung's ten sons by placing them in stocks in a clearing in the wild wood. One son is torn to pieces each night for nine nights by a Werewolf who is actually the witch-mother of the king. However, on the tenth night, Sigmund (with the help of his sister Signy) manages to trick the Werewolf and slays her by tearing out her tongue with his teeth.

Sigmund escapes and lives for many years as an outlaw in an underground house in the wild wood. Signy's desire for vengeance is so great that, while remaining the wife of the King of Gothland, she casts a spell on Sigmund. When she comes to his underground house, he does not know it is his own sister and makes love to her. Months later, Signy has a child from this incestuous union. He is called Sifjolti, and when he is grown, Signy sends him to Sigmund in the wild wood, so together they may avenge Volsung's death.

After many trials, including stealing and wearing Werewolf skins and being buried alive in a barrow grave, Sigmund and Sifjolti set fire to the great hall of the Goth king. Signy secretly returns Odin's sword to Sigmund, and all who attempt to escape the fire are slain. Seeing the Goth king and his kin slain, Signy confesses the price she has paid to exact her revenge, including incest with her brother, and leaps into the flames.

Sigmund returns with Sifjolti to his homeland and claims his father's throne as King of Hunland. He rules successfully for many years, although his son Sifjolti dies by poisoning. Shortly after King Sigmund marries the Princess Hjordis, two armies of Vikings ambush Sigmund. However, they fail to slay him because of his supernatural sword. Into the fray of battle comes an ancient, one-eyed warrior. When Sigmund strikes this old man's spear shaft with his sword, the blade shatters. Sigmund knows his doom has come. The ancient warrior can be none other than Odin. Sigmund's enemies strike him down.

Sigmund is given mortal wounds by his enemies, yet he does not despair for he has lived long and he knows that his queen is heavy with child. The dying Sigmund tells his wife she must take the shards of Odin's sword. For Sigmund knows the prophecy that he will sire a son who, with the sword reforged, will win a prize greater than that of any mortal man.

Sigmund's queen flees the battleground and after a long journey finds refuge in the Viking court of the King of the Sea Danes. There, the exiled queen gives birth to her son, Sigurd, and raises him in secret under the protection of the Danes.

Now in the realm of the Sea Danes is a master smith. He is called Regin, and from his long, toiling hours at the forge, his powerful body is hunched and stunted like a Dwarf's. Yet from his fire and forge comes much beauty in jewels and bright weapons. Swords, spears and axes shine with a bright sheen. None know their equal.

No one knows Regin's age or his past. He entered the land of the Danes before the memory of the oldest king. He is no lord of fighting men, but a smith and a master of other crafts as well. He is filled with the wisdom of runes, chess play, and the languages of many lands.

But Regin casts a cold eye on life, and none knows him as a friend. So the Sea-Dane King is much surprised when Regin fosters Sigurd and becomes his tutor. There never was a pupil like Sigurd, so quick and eager to learn. He is well taught by the smith in many arts and disciplines, though in the warrior's skills he excels most. Teacher and pupil are a strange pair. Some say Regin is too cold-tempered, and Sigurd born too hot. Whatever the reason, over the years of learning, master and apprentice never form a bond of love or close friendship.

Wise though Sigurd becomes with Regin's teaching, there is something in his blood that beckons him to learn matters that are even beyond the smith's teachings. So Sigurd often goes to the forest for many days of wandering. On one such solitary journey Sigurd meets an ancient man in a cape and a wide-brimmed slouch hat. The old man's bearded face has but one eye, and he uses a spear as a walking-stick. This man tells Sigurd he may choose whatever horse he wishes for himself from his herd in the meadow.

When Sigurd chooses a young grey stallion, the old man smiles.

'Well chosen. He is called Grani, meaning grey-coat, and he is as sleek as quicksilver and will grow to become the strongest and swiftest stallion ever to be ridden by a mortal man. For Grani's sire was the immortal Sleipnir, the eight-legged stallion of Asgard, who rides stormclouds over the world.'

Not long afterwards, Regin sends for the youth.

'You have grown large and strong, Sigurd. Now is the time for an adventure,' says Regin. 'I have a tale to tell.'

The two then go out onto the green grass before Regin's hall. By an oak tree there is a stone bench on which the smith settles, while the huge youth sits on the grass at his feet.

'Know me now, young Sigurd, for what I am. Not a man, but one born in a time before the first man entered the spheres of the world. This was a time almost before there was Time. Giants and Dwarfs were filled with terrible strength, and there were Magicians of such power that even the gods feared to walk alone across the lands of Midgard.

'In this time, the gods Odin, Honir and Loki went on an adventure into Midgard and dared to enter the land of my father, Hreidmar, the greatest

Magician of the Nine Worlds. On the first day, the three gods came to a stream and a deep pool. Resting a while, they soon saw a lithe brown otter swimming in the pool. Diving deep, the otter caught a silver salmon in its jaws and, reaching the far shore, struggled to drag his prize out of the water. It seemed an opportunity not to be missed. Without a word, Loki hurled a stone and broke the otter's skull.

'Loki rejoiced at having won both otter and salmon with a single stone. He went to the otter and skinned it. Taking up their double prize of salmon and otter skin, the three gods walked on until evening, when they came to a great hall upon a fair heath. This was Hreidmar the Magician's hall which stood on the Glittering Heath just above the dark forest called the Mirkwood.

'When the three gods entered the hall, they made a gift of the salmon and the otter skin to their host. The Magician immediately flew into a rage, and bound the gods at once with a deadly spell. Then he called to me, to bring my fire-forged chains of unbreakable iron; and he called to my brother, the mighty Fafnir, to bind these gods tightly with my chains and his pitiless strength. Once this was done, no one but the Magician-King might ever free those three gods.

'Although my father much admired my craft and Fafnir's strength, it was his third son that he loved best. This son was the Magician's eyes and ears. He was a shape-shifter who travelled often in many forms of bird and beast, and told my father what went on in the wide world. He was called Otter after his favourite guise.

'This was the reason for the Magician-King's terrible wrath. The otter that the gods slew at the pool, then unknowingly offered as a gift, was the flayed skin of their host's favourite son.

'For this outrage, the Magician was intent on the destruction of all three who slew his son. But Odin spoke persuasively, saying truthfully that Otter was slain in ignorance; and that in such cases, payment of weregild instead of blood was just and honourable compensation. Though much grieved, the Magician-King laid the terms.

'"Fill my son's skin with gold and cover him with it too. Do that and I will spare you," he demanded, grimly.

'Since Loki had cast the fatal stone, he was chosen to find the weregild, while the others remained bound. Odin advised him to quickly find the Dwarf Andvari who was renowned for his wealth. This hoard of gold he hid in a mountain cavern beneath a waterfall. Yet Odin warned that Andvari the Dwarf was also a shape-shifter who hid his identity. Most often, he took the form of a great pike who lived in the pool beneath the falls, so he might better guard his watery treasury door.

'Loki was not long in finding the waterfall. He stared hard into the clear pool and saw the great pike hiding in the eddies under the rocks. When he dragged the pike to the land, gasping it took on Andvari's true shape and begged for mercy. Loki was not gentle. He twisted the Dwarf until his screams drowned out the sound of the water. Finally Andvari gave up his golden treasure to Loki, but the Dwarf begged that he might be allowed to keep just one red-gold ring for himself. Guessing at the ring's importance, Loki snatched the ring from Andvari as well, and hurried on his way.

'Now this was the ring called Andvarinaut, which means "Andvari's loom", for by its power gold comes, and treasure increases ever more. This golden ring breeds gold, though this was but one of its powers; many of its other powers are unknown. This one small red-gold ring that Loki stole was worth all the rest of the treasure together.

'The Dwarf screamed after him: "I curse you for this! The ring and the treasure it spawned will carry my curse forever. All who possess the ring and its treasure for long will be destroyed!"

'Loki returned to the Magician's hall with the gold hoard and stuffed Otter's skin tight with it, and piled gold over all. The price in weregild seemed to be made, but the Magician-King looked keenly at the treasure and pointed to one whisker which still protruded. Loki smiled grimly then, and let fall the ring Andvarinaut which he had held back. The ring covered the last hair and the payment was made.

'The Magician-King packed up the treasure in great oak chests, but took the ring Andvarinaut and placed it on his hand. Then he released the bonds of his spell, commanded Fafnir and me to unlock the chains, and the gods were given safe passage out of his land.

'For a short time, all seemed well, but the mere sight of the ring was a torment to Fafnir. And so, one night Fafnir crept to our father's bed and cut his throat while he slept. He placed Andvari's ring on his own hand, then appeared at my bedside with his bloody dagger.

'"Come," he said, "I have need of you."

'Fearfully I did as I was told and dragged the treasure out across the Glittering Heath and beyond to a cavern under a mountain deep in the Mirkwood.

'"You make a good porter, my brother. You've earned your life, but little else. If you turn now and run, I will not slay you. Put this gold from your mind, for it shall never be left unguarded."

'So it was that Fafnir won the ring and the treasure of the Dwarf Andvari with the blood of our father. Over that treasure, he ever after brooded. Hateful lust has poisoned his heart and mind, and all who have come his way by chance or intent, he has murdered. For now his outward form has matched his inner evil, and he has become a serpent: a huge dragon, the mightiest of this or any age.'

Sigurd now sees his destiny and takes up Regin's challenge.

'Slay me this dragon to avenge my father, and win for yourself great glory,' commands Regin. 'Help me to my share of the weregild, and besides glory you shall have Andvari's ring and the greater part of the treasure, as well.'

For such a mission, the valiant Sigurd desires a weapon to match his strength, and so goes to his mother and claims the shards of his father's sword that had been the gift of Odin. These shards he gives to Regin in his smithy. Regin sets furiously to work, heating them in the hottest fire, reforging the blade and tempering it in the blood of a bull. The sacred runes above the hilt recover their brightness, the rings engraved on the steel gleam like silver, and as the smith carries the sword out into the daylight, it seems that flames play along its edge.

Sigurd takes the weapon in his strong hands and swings it fiercely at the smith's anvil. The sword slices clean through the iron and the wooden stock below it, as well. Yet the blade is unnotched by the stroke.

'This truly can be no other but the sword called Gram, the gift of Odin, which my father swore would one day be reforged and be given to his only son,' says Sigurd, smiling.

So armed and mounted on his steed Grani, Sigurd rides on his quest with Regin. They come at last to the fire-scorched and desolate outlands of what was once the Glittering Heath. Now this place is wild and blasted heath on the edge of the evil forest of Mirkwood. It is a scorched wasteland where many a hero was slain by the dragon. Upon this heath is cut a deep path of stone that is the slime-filled track of a dragon road. The road leads to Fafnir's serpent cavern deep in the Mirkwood. There the dragon made his bed upon the golden treasure that was the ring-hoard of Andvari the Dwarf. Fafnir left his golden bed only once each day when he travelled his road to the foul pool on the heath

where he drank
at dusk.

'Dig a trench in
the dragon's path and
hide in it,' advises Regin.
'When he comes over you
thrust your sword up into his
soft belly. You cannot fail.'

While Sigurd is digging, Regin makes
off across the heath and hides himself in the
Mirkwood. A shadow falls over the pit and
Sigurd whirls around. It is the same one-eyed,
bearded old man who had given Sigurd his grey
horse.

'Small wisdom, short life,' murmurs the old man, leaning
on his spear. 'The dragon's blood will sear your bones. Dig
several pits, and hide in the one to the left. Then you may thrust your
blade into the worm's heart, while the boiling, poison blood falls into
another pit.'

By evening the work is done, and just in time. The stinking dragon comes
down to drink, roaring horribly and slavering poison over the ground. Biding
his time, Sigurd thrusts Gram's blade into the dragon's breast up to the hilt.
The scalding, corrosive blood floods into the ditch, and Fafnir collapses. His
writhing coils shake the earth, his roaring fills the air with flame and venom. His
jaws snap at an enemy he cannot reach, as he curses the hero who has slain him
and the brother who betrayed him.

When Sigurd emerges from his pit, Regin too comes from his hiding-place
and feigns both sorrow and joy. Claiming that he wishes to remove any blood
guilt from Sigurd for the slaying of Fafnir, Regin asks Sigurd to cut the dragon's
heart from its body and roast it. Regin claims that by eating the dragon's heart,
he alone might be brought to account for its death.

Sigurd does as Regin tells him and builds a fire and spits the heart over the
flames. But as the dragon's heart cooks, its juice spits out and scalds the young
man's fingers. He puts his fingers in his mouth and, upon tasting the monster's
heartblood, at once finds he can understand the language of the birds in the
trees about him.

The birds speak with sorrow, for they know of Regin's treachery. How the
smith will gain great wisdom and bravery by eating the dragon's heart, then
plans to slay Sigurd in his sleep. The birds know that Regin will never share the

golden treasure, nor the ring with the brave youth, despite his sworn oath. They know as well that Regin wishes to steal Sigurd's sword and steed.

Hearing this talk among the birds, Sigurd moves swiftly. With his sword Gram, he strikes the false smith's head from his shoulders. Then, Sigurd eats the dragon's heart himself and sets to work clearing out Fafnir's lair.

It is a whole day's work, for the cave floor is carpeted with drifts of gold. No three horses could have stood beneath such a load, but Grani carries this with ease. The extra burden of Sigurd, now wearing golden armour, seems to cause him no effort at all.

So laden, with the Ring of Andvari on his hand, Sigurd the Dragonslayer goes out of that burnt wasteland in search of more adventures. He seeks and achieves further honour, for he makes war on all the kings and princes who murdered his father and his kinsmen, and slays them every one.

Many other adventures the youth has as well, but then he goes south into the Lands of the Franks. Travelling long one night he sees, like a beacon, a great ring of flames on a mountain ridge. The next morning he climbs that ridge called the Hindfell where he sees a stone tower in the midst of the ring of flames.

Sigurd does not hesitate. He urges Grani into the ring of fire. Nor does Grani flinch. His leap is as high as it is long, and though his tail and mane are scorched,

he stands quietly once they are through. There is an inner circle next: an overlapping ring of massive war shields, their bases fixed in the mountain rock. Sigurd draws Gram and shears a path through the iron wall of shields.

Beyond this is a stone tower, and within it is

the body of a warrior on a bier. Or so it seems. When Sigurd takes the helmet from the warrior's head, he sees that this is a woman and that she is not dead, but sleeping. As he gazes on her, Sigurd sees she is of a warrior's stature and a woman's grace. He also sees a buckthorn protruding from her neck. When Sigurd draws it out, this sleeping beauty sighs and wakes. The shield maiden's steady grey eyes look up at him with love.

This sleeping beauty is Brynhild who was once a Valkyrie, one of Odin's own battle maidens – his beautiful angels of death – who gathered the souls of heroes as they fell in war and carried them to Valhalla. But once, she set her will against Odin in the matter of a man's life. For this Odin pierced her with a sleep-thorn and set her in a tower surrounded by a ring of fire.

Only a hero who did not know fear would be able to pass through the ring of fire. When Brynhild opens her eyes, she knows Sigurd for the hero he is, and Sigurd knows that in the Valkyrie he has his match for courage and his master in wisdom.

When Sigurd becomes the Valkyrie's lover, within the ring of fire, he learns what twenty lifetimes might never teach a mortal man. For in that embrace of love, many things in Sigurd are awakened and filled with the wisdom of the gods; while in Brynhild many things are put to sleep, and filled with the unknowing of mortals.

Sigurd, as the lover of the Valkyrie, knows that he must embrace strife and war which give a warrior immortal fame. Painful as it is, Sigurd knows he must leave Brynhild and go out of the ring of fire into the world of men again where he might earn glory enough to be worthy of his bride. This Sigurd resolves to do, but as a token of his eternal love and as a promise of his return, he places the Ring of Andvari – that all the world desired – upon Brynhild's hand. While Brynhild sleeps, Sigurd rises at dawn, mounts Grani and passes out of the ring of fire.

When Brynhild wakes, she remembers nothing of Sigurd, or Odin, or any of her past before that day. Upon her hand is a gold ring, though she does not know its reason. All she knows is that she must await the coming of a warrior who knows no fear and can pass through the ring of fire. To this man, and this man alone, she will be sworn in marriage.

As for Sigurd, great though his love is for Brynhild, he knows that his fate is that of a warrior. Like his father, he has been chosen by Odin, and in his service Sigurd travels to many lands, and slays no less than five mighty kings in battle.

In time, Sigurd comes to the Rhinelands which are ruled over by the King of the Nibelungs. The Nibelung King welcomes the now famous hero, Sigurd the

Dragonslayer, with great warmth and friendship. In time, Sigurd and the king's three sons – Gunnar, Hogni and Guttorm – become the closest of friends and allies in both war and peace. Sigurd and Gunnar swear unbreakable oaths of friendship, and become blood-brothers.

Seeing how Sigurd the Dragonslayer's friendship has so increased the power and wealth of their realm, Gunnar's mother Grimhild, the Queen of the Nibelungs, wishes to keep him within their realm. To this end, she hopes Sigurd might marry her daughter, the beautiful Gudrun. However, though she knows Gudrun loves Sigurd, she also knows Sigurd loves another.

Grimhild's wish is not hopeless. For Queen of the Nibelungs though she is, Grimhild is also secretly a great witch capable of casting spells and making powerful potions. So in the feasting-hall one evening, Grimhild gives to Sigurd an enchanted drink. This potion robs Sigurd of his memory of the Valkyrie whom he swore to love always, and at the same time fills him with desire for the beautiful Gudrun.

Obedient to the spell, Sigurd soon asks for Gudrun's hand and their marriage is blessed by all who lived in the Rhinelands. Many seasons pass, the royal couple are happy, and the power and glory of the Nibelungs grows and grows. Yet tales of a strange and beautiful maiden held captive in a ring of fire on a mountain reach the court. These tales mean nothing to Sigurd, but Gunnar wishes to win this maiden and make her his queen. His mother, Grimhild, is wary of this adventure and asks Sigurd to go with his blood-brother. Sigurd does this gladly, but Grimhild also gives to Sigurd a potion. By the potion's power Sigurd may change his appearance to that of Gunnar.

Gunnar and Sigurd ride away and at last come to Hindfell and the mountain with the tower ringed in fire. Gunnar sets his spurs to his horse, but the beast turns away at each attempt, and the flames rear higher and more fiercely at every failure. Even though Sigurd lets him mount Grani, Gunnar gets nowhere.

Gunnar despairs at ever winning his queen, so he begs Sigurd to try in his place. Sigurd uses Grimhild's potion and changes his appearance to that of Gunnar. He then mounts Grani and charges straight into the ring of fire. Sigurd's boots catch fire and Grani's mane and tail are alight. Horse and rider seem to hang in that inferno forever, deafened and blinded by its heat, but finally they pass through the flames.

Next is the barrier of the wall of shields, but as before, Sigurd shears through the iron wall with his sword. Behind this wall in the tower sits the beauty that is Brynhild all in white upon a crested throne, like a proud swan borne up on a foaming wave.

'What man are you?' asks Brynhild of the one standing before her. Memories of her past are gone from her mind, yet something deep within her tells her something is wrong.

'My name is Gunnar the Nibelung,' says the rider, 'and I claim you as my queen.' Passing through the ring of fire was the price of Brynhild's hand, and she cannot refuse such a hero. Nor is there any reason for her to do so, for the man before her is handsome enough; and – by virtue of his deed – is brave beyond the measure of other mortals.

So does Brynhild embrace him and place her gold Ring of Andvari upon his hand to pledge her eternal love. Then within the tower she takes him to bed and lays with him for three nights, though these nights were strange to her. For each night the hero places his long sword on the bed between them. He must do this, he says, for he will not make love to his new queen until they both return to the great halls of the Nibelungs. In this way, the disguised Sigurd conspires, so he might not betray Gunnar and dishonour his bride.

When the marriage of Brynhild and Gunnar takes place in the hall of the Nibelungs, it is the true Gunnar who weds Brynhild and takes her to bed. In the land of the Nibelungs all seems content. But one day while bathing in a stream the two young queens set to quarrelling. Brynhild boasts that Gunnar is a greater man than Sigurd by virtue of his feat of passing through the ring of fire.

Gudrun will have none of this, for Sigurd has foolishly told to his wife the true tale of that adventure. So, the young queen cruelly reveals that truth to Brynhild; and as proof shows her the gold ring upon her hand. By this Brynhild is crushed, for this was the Ring Andvarinaut that she thought she had given to Gunnar that day on the mountain, but in fact Sigurd had taken and given to his own wife.

Now all the secrets are out, and poison runs in Brynhild's heart when she learns of how she has been deceived. Outraged, she can only think of vengeance. Brynhild turns to Gunnar and his brothers Hogni and Guttorm. She taunts and threatens her husband.

'All the people now laugh and say I have married a coward,' mocks Brynhild. 'And my disgrace is your disgrace, for they say not only did another man win your wife for you, but also took your place in the wedding bed. And no use is there to deny this, for the Ring of Andvari – which Sigurd gave your sister – is proof that this is so.'

'Sigurd shall die, then. Or I shall,' swears Gunnar. But he has neither the heart nor the courage to act himself, and slay his friend. Instead he and Hogni inflame the heart of their youngest brother, Guttorm, with promises and Grimhild's potions to slay Sigurd.

That night Guttorm creeps into the chamber where Sigurd lies sleeping in Gudrun's arms. Young Guttorm thrusts his sword down with such force that it pierces the man and the bedstead too. Waking to death, Sigurd still finds strength enough to snatch up Gram and hurl it after his killer. The terrible sword in flight severs the youth in half as he reaches the door. Guttorm's legs fall forward, but his torso drops back into the room.

When Brynhild hears Gudrun's scream she laughs aloud, but there is no joy in her terrible revenge. For that night, Brynhild takes Sigurd's sword and slays herself. True to her Valkyrie passion, she resolves that if she cannot be wed to Sigurd in life she will be wed to him in death. Once again and finally, Sigurd and Brynhild lie side by side – with Odin's bright sword between them – as the fierce flames of their funeral pyre slowly devour them.

So ends the life of Sigurd the Dragonslayer, but this is not the end of the tale of the Ring of Andvari, nor of the Dwarf's treasure. For the ring remains on Gudrun's hand and the treasure is taken by her brothers Gunnar and Hogni, and hidden by them in a secret cavern in the River Rhine.

Gudrun is filled with horror at Sigurd's death at the hands of her brothers, but she does not grieve long before her mother Grimhild comes to comfort her. Once again the old witch has prepared a potion which secretly she gives to Gudrun to make her forget her grief, and the evil her brothers have done. Instead the potion fills her with love and loyalty to her brothers in all matters.

Still, Gunnar and Hogni wish to have Gudrun gone. They also wish to increase the power and glory of the Nibelungs, and believe they might do so by an alliance with the mighty Atli, the King of the Huns. And so, the brothers send Gudrun to Atli. Gudrun likes it not, but obeys and weds the King of the Huns and is his queen.

Now Atli the Hun is a powerful man, but one who is filled with greed. He has heard much of the huge treasure that Sigurd the Dragonslayer once won, and that the Nibelungs have taken this hoard by a foul murder. Each time Gudrun walks before Atli, her gold ring glints and Atli finds he can think of nothing else but that golden treasure.

Time passes and Gudrun gives the Hun King two young sons, but all the while Atli plans an intrigue and finally he acts. King Atli invites Gunnar and Hogni and all the Nibelung nobles to a great feast in his mead hall. But when the Nibelungs come to the feast hall, they soon discover that a huge army of Huns has surrounded them. The great feast hall becomes a slaughterhouse. Although the Nibelungs slay ten for every one they lose, finally they are overwhelmed and all are murdered, save the brothers Gunnar and Hogni. These two are bound with chains and held captive.

The Hun King has Gunnar brought before him in chains, and promises to spare his life if he will give up the golden treasure that was taken from Sigurd the Volsung. But Gunnar says that he and Hogni have hidden the treasure in a secret cavern beneath the Rhine, and swore blood oaths that neither will reveal it while the other lives. At once Atli gives an order, and within the hour a soldier returns. In his hand is Hogni's heart which has been torn from his living breast.

Gunnar greets this loathsome act with cruel laughter. There had been no oath, he explains. Gunnar had been fearful that Hogni might surrender the treasure to save his life. But now that his brother is slain, only Gunnar knows the secret, and he will never surrender it. In rage, Atli has Gunnar bound and cast in a pit where serpents filled with venom finally still that warrior's stubborn heart.

The Hun King's wife, Queen Gudrun, is filled with grief at the death of her brothers and the obliteration of the Nibelungs. Although Andvari's treasure is lost, Andvari's ring still carries the Dwarf's curse while it remains on Gudrun's hand. And Gudrun – as the last of the Nibelungs – resolves to have bloody retribution for Atli's treachery.

Though the battle with the Nibelungs cost Atli dearly and profited him little, the Hun King calls for a victory feast in his great hall. Secretly, Gudrun makes her preparations. She murders her own two children, Atli's sons. From their skulls, she makes two cups. Their innocent blood she mixes with the wine; and their hearts and entrails she spits and roasts as his meat. All this she serves up to Atli at the feast.

Then late that night, Gudrun takes a knife and cuts the Hun King's throat while he sleeps. She then creeps away, bars all the doors from without, and sets the Hun King's great hall to the torch. This is the greatest pyre that has ever been seen in the land of the Huns, for all Atli's soldiers and vassals perish in their sleep in that fire.

Before that inferno, Gudrun stands and stares with mounting madness, the flames bringing back many terrible memories. She flees the Hunlands and wanders until she comes to a high cliff overlooking the sea. She looks one more time at the glinting gold Ring of Andvari on her hand, then with a sigh she fills her apron with stones and leaps into the sea.

CHAPTER SIX

ARTHURIAN LEGENDS

In *The Lord of the Rings*, Tolkien's heroes Aragorn and Gandalf are most commonly linked in the popular imagination with the tales of King Arthur and Merlin the Magician. This is in part because King Arthur is without doubt Britain's most famous legendary hero. The stature of Arthur through many popular retellings has made him the very embodiment of British virtues and strengths.

Historically, the legends of King Arthur were almost unknown until the twelfth century, but they abounded throughout the courts of Europe by the fourteenth century. Among the first books ever printed in Britain was the Caxton-Malory *Le Morte d'Arthur*, which brought the Arthurian cycle to the English language in written form – for although many other authors wrote various legends of Arthur in manuscript, most did so in the official court language of French.

The historical basis for King Arthur is very slim. The likely model for Arthur was probably the Romanized Celt, Ambrosius Aurelianus. By later accounts he was known by the name Artorius and the Roman title of Dux Bellorum. Between AD 493 and 516, Artorius was said to have led the Britons against the Saxons in twelve great battles, culminating in the victory of Mons Badonicus. In time, the warrior-king figure of Arthur attracted the oral traditions of both Celt and Saxon bards as a symbol of a brief romantic age of order and stability. When order and stability of a particularly stern and ruthless kind was established by William the Conqueror and his Norman knights, the figure of King Arthur grew to even greater stature. Arthur was the chosen ancestral hero of the British people who saw in him a noble king who ruled a courtly, idealized world. In King Arthur and his Knights of the Round Table, the British looked back in pride to a past age of greatness.

English-language readers of *The Lord of the Rings* frequently register the undeniable connection between Arthur and Aragorn, and Merlin and Gandalf. However, what is often not clear to many is that the Arthurian romances are themselves largely based on earlier Teutonic myths and legends. Although the Arthurian legends make their own unique contributions, in many respects it is even more important to see the connection between Aragorn and Sigurd, and Gandalf and Odin.

Although the archetypal figures of hero and wizard are clearly similar in pagan saga, medieval legend and modern fantasy, the context for all three is very different. The creation of a medieval King Arthur and a court based roughly on Christian moral principles naturally resulted in considerable reshaping of many of the fiercer aspects of the early pagan hero tradition. The saga hero Sigurd is a wild beast of a warrior who clearly would not even get a dinner invitation to Arthur's courtly round table. Curiously, although Tolkien's world is a pagan, pre-religious one, his hero requires quite as much reshaping as Arthur because of his concept of absolute good and evil. Although Tolkien's Aragorn is a pagan hero, he is often even more upright and moral than the medieval Christian King Arthur.

The comparison of the three heroes – Arthur, Sigurd and Aragorn – demonstrates the power of archetypes in dictating aspects of character in the heroes of legend and myth. If we look at the lives of each of these three, we see certain life patterns that are identical.

Arthur, Sigurd and Aragorn are all orphaned sons and rightful heirs to kings slain in battle. All are deprived of their inherited kingdoms, and are in danger of assassination. All are the last of their dynasty, and their noble lineage will end if they are slain. All are raised secretly in foster homes under the protection of a foreign noble who is a distant relative. Arthur is raised in the castle of Sir Ector; Sigurd in the hall of King Hjalprek; and Aragorn in the house of Master Elrond Halfelven. During their fostering – in childhood and as youths – all three achieve feats of strength and skill that mark them for future greatness.

All three heroes fall in love with beautiful maidens, but all must overcome several seemingly impossible obstacles before they may marry: Arthur to Guinevere, Sigurd to Brynhild, Aragorn to Arwen. Each of these lovers is to some degree tragic heroines: Guinevere becomes a nun and dies in a convent, Brynhild loses her supernatural Valkyrie power and commits suicide, and Arwen sacrifices her Elven immortality and dies a human death. The most obvious difference between King Arthur and Sigurd appears to be the object of their respective quests. The great quest tradition usually associated with King Arthur is not the Ring, but the Quest for the Holy Grail. The 'grail' is the chalice that was used by Christ at the Last Supper, and also the same cup with which Joseph of Arimathea caught the blood that flowed from the side of the crucified Saviour.

The story of the Grail is a very late addition to the Arthurian romance cycle. It has been said that it was Richard Wagner's genius to recognize the Ring as the Grail Quest of his race. In fact the reverse is true, as Wagner himself recognized when he wrote his Grail Quest opera *Parsifal*. Wagner found that the Holy Grail was a Christianized retelling of the ring quest. In *Parsifal*, the Ring mysteriously ascends and is transformed into the Holy Grail.

Both Richard Wagner and Alfred Lord Tennyson in his epic Arthurian poem 'Idylls of the King' saw the Holy Grail as the exclusively spiritual aspects of the ring quest. The Grail Quest became a disaster for those who pursued it for the opposite reasons to those determining that the Ring was a disaster for others.

In the ring quests of both *The Lord of the Rings* and 'The Volsunga Saga', there is a sense that those who possessed these rings were destroyed by their own desire for earthly wealth and power. Tolkien's Ringwraiths, for instance, acquired their Rings of Power to make themselves rich and powerful, by selling their souls. Ultimately, however, the ring's mastery of the world is an illusion. The ring eventually comes to enslave its owner. It is the old moral question: 'What does it profit a man to win all the world, if he lose his soul?' You can't own anything if you don't own your soul.

What happened with the quest for the Holy Grail was the opposite. The Grail Quest was essentially a spiritual journey by a soul which could only be completed if all the corrupting influences of the body and the material world were rejected. The problem is that no being can exist on a purely spiritual level, and still remain within the mortal world. Consequently, when the Round Table's knights took on a quest that required the spiritual virtues of a saint, the result was a disaster that all but destroyed Arthur's mortal kingdom. If the ring quest required a pact with demons at the cost of one's immortal soul, the Grail Quest was a pact with angels at the cost of one's mortal body.

Simply stated, the Grail Quest is the medieval Christian image chosen to show the spiritual aspect of the ring quest. One might illustrate the point by saying that the gold ring that ascends to heaven becomes a halo, while the gold ring that descends to earth becomes a crown. The exclusive pursuit of either aspect ends in tragedy: the needs of the spirit and body must both be satisfied. One cannot survive without the other.

The Grail Quest aside, the Arthurian legends do have a quest for a ring which is critical to the security of Arthur's kingdom. However, the medieval Christian and chivalric tradition somewhat changes its nature. The ring that is the object of Arthur's quest is the gold marriage ring of his beloved Queen Guinevere. To make himself a worthy suitor, Arthur slays twelve troublesome giants and conquers twelve feuding kings. To give his Queen a worthy realm, Arthur reclaims his rightful kingdom, and makes alliances with all other worthy barons and knights of the land as well.

This achieved, King Arthur and Queen Guinevere are wed and a sacred oath is sworn upon the marriage ring. It is a marriage of true love, but it is also a political marriage. Emblematically, Queen Guinevere brings the Round Table as part of her dowry to Camelot. Around this great table, an iron ring of knights is forged by the swearing of oaths to the King and the Queen. The iron ring will survive as long as the oath sworn upon the gold marriage ring remains unbroken.

In *The Lord of the Rings*, the One Ring is evil; in 'The Volsunga Saga', the Ring of Andvari is cursed. In the Arthurian tradition, the gold ring is good so long as the oath sworn on it is true. However, whatever the origin of the rings, false oaths sworn on them do not go unpunished.

The Volsung and Nibelung downfalls result directly from Sigurd's unwitting violation of the oath he swore to Brynhild when he gave her the Ring of Andvari as a pledge of eternal love. When Sigurd unknowingly breaks that oath, disaster consumes them all. Similarly, the breaking of the sacred oath sworn on the marriage ring of Arthur and Guinevere – through the Queen's adultery with Sir Lancelot – results in the break-up of the Round Table. The iron ring of the knights is broken. Chaos and anarchy are let loose, and the kingdom destroyed. Both traditions read the curse of the ring in the same way: the house built on a lie cannot survive.

In *The Lord of the Rings*, the One Ring is itself evil. A master of disguise, Sauron goes among the Elven-smiths of Eregion with many false promises about creating rings of good virtue and enchantment. So completely does Sauron deceive the Elves that unknowingly they help him forge the Rings of Power. Only then does Sauron secretly go to his smithy in Mount Doom. There, using all the false promises and lies invented by sorcerers since the dawn of time, Sauron forges the One Ring with which he seeks to fetter and enslave the world.

The centre of Sauron's evil empire is the Dark Tower of Mordor, and the massive foundation of the tower is built through the power of the One Ring.

However, when the One Ring is destroyed in the fires of Mount Doom, the illusion of Sauron's power vanishes. Sauron's 'house' in the form of the Dark Tower is built on the monstrous lies of the One Ring and cannot survive. The foundations crumble. The Ring Lord and all his servants are reduced to smoke and ash carried away on a desolate wind. The Dark Tower collapses into a heap of rubble and dust.

Beyond the ring quest motif itself, there are many other points of comparison between the saga, the romance and the fantasy. Tolkien's hero Aragorn in many ways resembles both Arthur and Sigurd; in some ways, one or the other.

The heritage of the sword of the warrior-king is naturally enough critical to all three heroes. Arthur proves his right to the sword in a famous contest: he alone is able to pull the sword from the stone. This is an act that duplicates the contest in the Volsunga Saga, when Sigurd's father Sigmund alone can draw the sword Odin has driven into the oak tree, Branstock. However, neither Sigurd nor Aragorn are presented with such contests. They are both given their swords as heirlooms; their problem is that both swords are broken, and neither may use the swords and reclaim their kingdoms until they are reforged. In Sigurd's case, the sword was broken by the Wizard Odin in his father Sigmund's last battle, while Aragorn's sword was broken by his ancestor Elendil in his last battle with the Wizard Sauron.

Like the heirloom swords of Sigurd and Aragorn, Arthur's sword is supposedly unbreakable; but through special circumstances, all three are broken. Sigmund's and Aragorn's swords break in battles with supernatural opponents, while King Arthur's sword breaks when he makes an unrighteous attack on Sir Pellinore. It seems the Christian King's sword is endowed with a moral conscience. Sir Pellinore is on the point of killing Arthur when Merlin appears and puts Pellinore into a deep swoon. Thus, Arthur's weapon is broken but he is not slain as Sigmund was when his weapon broke. Arthur is saved by the Wizard Merlin; he undergoes a spiritual resurrection. The penitent and reformed Arthur is reborn; as – in a sense – Sigmund is resurrected in his son Sigurd; and Elendil is resurrected in his descendant Aragorn.

Once Sigurd reforges his sword Gram, he sets out at once to reclaim his heritage. He does this by avenging his father's death and reclaiming his kingdom by conquest, slaying the dragon Fafnir and winning the monster's treasure and golden ring. Sigurd then goes on to win his beloved Valkyrie princess Brynhild. To some degree, although the ring quest is different (the aim being destruction rather than winning), Aragorn's life mirrors Sigurd's. Once Aragorn's sword Andúril is reforged, he sets off to reclaim his heritage. He avenges his father's death, reclaims his kingdom by conquest, and after the destruction of the One Ring, wins his beloved Elven princess Arwen.

The dragon-slaying element of the Sigurd tale is not present in *The Lord of the Rings*, but is taken up by Tolkien in *The Hobbit*. Although the dragon-slayer is rather secondary to the main characters in the story of *The Hobbit*, the heroic pattern is almost identical to the tale of Sigurd the Dragonslayer. The dispossessed exile, Bard the Bowman, is a descendant of the Kings of Dale whom the dragon Smaug the Golden slew and robbed of their gold. Bard has no sword but a black arrow as an heirloom. Understanding the language of birds, Bard learns the secret of the dragon's unarmoured belly and pierces his heart with his black arrow. Bard avenges his father and ancestors, slays the dragon and wins the treasure. He then re-establishes his kingdom and marries his queen.

The nature of Aragorn's sword owes something to both the Arthurian and Volsung traditions. Aragorn's sword was originally named Narsil, meaning 'red and white flame', and was forged by the greatest of all Dwarf-smiths, Telchar the Smith. Narsil is broken by Elendil at the end of the Second Age, and is reforged by the Elven-smiths of Rivendell for Aragorn. It is then renamed Andúril, meaning the 'flame of the west', and its blade glows red in sunlight and white in moonlight.

In the Volsung tradition, the sword Odin drives into the tree and Sigmund wins was forged by the greatest of the Elf-smiths of Alfheim, Volund, whom the Saxons called Wayland the Smith. This sword of Odin has no formal name until it is reforged by the Dwarf-like smith Regin for Sigurd. The sword is then named Gram and its blade is distinguished by the blue flames that play along its razor edges.

King Arthur differs from Sigurd and Aragorn in that he does not have his broken sword reforged. The sword is simply replaced by another, even more extraordinary sword. Arthur is given his new sword 'Excalibur' by the enchantress Vivien, who is also known as the mystical Lady of the Lake. In *The Lord of the Rings*, Vivien is comparable to the Elf Queen Galadriel of Lothlórien. The Elf Queen's gift is not a sword, but a jewelled sheath that makes the sword blade unstainable and unbreakable.

Excalibur also has a jewelled scabbard, but it is blessed with a spell to the effect that, so long as Arthur wears it, he can lose no blood, no matter how badly wounded. The blade of Arthur's Excalibur is equal to the other weapons and glows with supernatural light. In battle, it is said to give off the light of thirty torches. Like Gram and Andúril, it can cleave through iron and stone, yet maintain its razor edge.

Perhaps the most telling connection between the three heroes is displayed in the similarity of their mentors: Merlin, Odin and Gandalf. All to some degree fit the archetypal form of the Wizard. All are non-human beings gifted with supernatural powers and prophetic skills. All are counsellors of future kings in peace and war, yet have no interest in worldly power themselves. In a sense they are all vehicles of fate who guide the hero. All are similar in appearance: vital, old wanderers of great learning with long white beards. They all carry a Wizard's staff and wear a broad-brimmed hat and long robes.

In many aspects of his personality, Gandalf is rather more like Merlin than Odin. Odin was, of course, an immortal god who went among the mortals of Midgard as an ancient traveller. Originally Merlin was in all likelihood an old Celtic god who similarly visited mortals in this Wizard form, although later traditions claimed he was the offspring of a mortal and an Elf or Demon. Gandalf's origins are as a demi-god who is chosen as one of five Istari or Wizards who come to Middle-earth to live among the mortals.

In many of his powers, however, Gandalf is far more like the Nordic Odin than the Celtic Merlin. To begin with his, name comes from the *Prose Edda*, and literally means 'Sorcerer-Elf'. In his use of runes, incantations, and even his Wizard powers, Gandalf is more comparable to Odin. Even Gandalf's horse comes directly from Norse traditions. 'Shadowfax' means 'silver-grey' and closely resembles Grani, 'the Grey' steed of Sigurd. Grani, who understood human speech, was the silver-grey offspring of Odin's supernatural eight-legged horse, Sleipnir. Shadowfax, who also understands the language of Men, is one of the Mearas, a race of horses descended from the god Oromë the Hunter's supernatural horse, Nahar.

Once their work as mentors and advisers to the heroes is done, all the Wizards mysteriously depart. All three Wizards – Odin, Merlin, Gandalf – pass out of mortal realms rather than die. Odin, after advising his heroes, wanders out of the mortal world, and (after a pilgrimage to Hel) finally ascends the Rainbow Bridge to the immortal kingdom of the gods in Asgard. Merlin wanders away on a solitary pilgrimage, never to return, for he is caught up in an enchantment and lives in a dreaming trance in – according to varying traditions – a tomb, a tree, or a tower on an island in the western sea.

Tolkien's Gandalf takes elements from both Odin's and Merlin's tales by having a double fate. As Gandalf the Grey, after his battle with the Balrog of Moria, he falls into the bowels of the earth where he remains in a death-like, yet dreaming, state. When he is resurrected as Gandalf the White, he meets his second end on Middle-earth, when he sails on an Elven ship to the immortal kingdom of the gods in Aman over the western sea.

The end of Gandalf on Middle-earth with the departure of the Ringbearers in the white Elven ship from the Grey Havens is also the end of Tolkien's epic novel. In looking for Arthurian elements in *The Lord of the Rings*, there can be no doubt that the novel's bittersweet ending is consciously modelled on the tales of Arthur's death.

It is an ending that is derived from the Celtic side of King Arthur's tradition, rather than his Teutonic one. After his final battle, the mortally wounded Arthur is taken on a mysterious barge by a beautiful Faerie Queen. The barge carries the wounded king westward across the water to the faerie land of Avalon, where Arthur will be healed and given immortal life.

This end to Arthur's mortal life is very like the end of *The Lord of the Rings*. However, it is important to point out that this is not Aragorn's end. Aragorn remains to die within the mortal world. The supreme reward of this voyage into the land of immortals is reserved for another. The 'wounded king' who sails on the Elf Queen Galadriel's ship across the western sea, past the Elven towers of Avallónë, is not Aragorn. It is Frodo the Hobbit Ringbearer, who is rightly the real hero of *The Lord of the Rings*.

Frodo's adventures appear at first to be a foil to Aragorn's great deeds. The diminutive Hobbit is too frail and all too human to appear initially as a likely candidate for the occupation of questing hero. Aragorn, on the other hand, is large, strong, bold – and almost inhuman in his bravery and virtue. However, in the end, it is the human qualities of the Hobbit that are finally what is required to prevail in the quest. The deep wisdom of compassion found in the human (or Hobbit) heart succeeds where heroic strength cannot.

Curiously, throughout *The Lord of the Rings* and *The Hobbit*, although they appear to be a comic foil to the larger heroic personalities of the Men and Elves, nearly all the greatest deeds are achieved, or are caused to be achieved, by the Hobbits. Bilbo's adventures result in the death of Smaug the Dragon and he finds the One Ring. Meriadoc kills the Witch-king of Morgul, and with Peregrin motivates the Ents who destroy Saruman's Tower. Samwise mortally wounds the giant Shelob the Spider and, most important of all, Frodo (with Gollum) destroys Sauron and the One Ring in Mordor.

In the end, the Hobbits are the real heroes. It is humble Frodo Baggins, not the noble Aragorn, who achieves the ring quest. He does so at the cost of his health through the loss of a finger and a poisoned wound that will not heal. The wounded Hobbit – like the wounded Arthur – is taken to be supernaturally healed. It is not Aragorn the King, but Frodo – the hero of the heart – who is chosen to sail to the land of the immortals.

CHAPTER SEVEN

CAROLINGIAN LEGENDS

As King Arthur became the national hero of Britain around whom a great cycle of legends grew, so on the Continent the historical figure of the Holy Roman Emperor Charlemagne grew into one of the great figures of romance. As with Arthur's knights, Charlemagne's legends included the many tales of his paladins. The adventures of these Christian knights allied to Charlemagne were told in the famous 'Chansons de geste'.

Tolkien himself often pointed out how many readers saw the connection between Aragorn and King Arthur, but he found that they usually missed the connection between Aragorn and Charlemagne. Certainly, it seemed to him, Aragorn's great task of forging the Reunited Kingdom of Arnor and Gondor from the ruins of the ancient Dúnedain empire after more than a millennium of barbarian chaos was historically parallel to Charlemagne's task of creating the Holy Roman Empire from the ruins of the ancient Roman empire.

Geographically, as well, Tolkien saw that the extent of the Reunited Kingdom of his epic far more closely paralleled the expanse of Charlemagne's realm. The action of *The Lord of the Rings* takes place in the north-west of a Middle-earth in a region roughly equivalent to the European landmass. Hobbiton and Rivendale, as Tolkien often acknowledged, were roughly intended to be on the latitude of Oxford. By his own estimations, this put Gondor and Minas Tirith some six hundred miles to the south in a location that might be equivalent to Florence. Rather than seeing *The Lord of the Rings* as being inspired entirely by

71

Arthurian or Norse models, Tolkien suggested (in a letter written in 1967): 'the progress of the tale ends in what is far more like the re-establishment of an effective Holy Roman Empire with its seat in Rome.'

Certainly, the scale of Charlemagne's undertaking to create a Holy Roman Empire was more like the challenge that faced Aragorn on Middle-earth than that of King Arthur. The parallel is fairly obvious. In *The Lord of the Rings*, we learn that the once United Númenórean Kingdom is split into the two weakened and deteriorating realms of the north and south, Arnor and Gondor. This is comparable to the historical Roman Empire which was split into two weakened and deteriorating realms of the east and the west, Rome and Byzantium. It is certain that Tolkien himself considered such a parallel, writing that he saw Gondor at the time of the War of the Ring as 'a kind of proud, venerable, but increasingly impotent Byzantium.'

The power and variety of Charlemagne's enemies were similar to those Aragorn fought in his struggle to reforge the ancient Númenórean Kingdoms. As Aragorn had to fight a powerful enemy to the south in the form of the Southrons of Harad, so Charlemagne had a similar foe in the form of the Saracens of Spain and North Africa. To the east, Aragorn had the Easterling tribes and barbarian hordes who worshipped the evil eye of Sauron the Dark Lord; while on Charlemagne's eastern frontier were the Germanic tribes and barbarian hordes who worshipped the one-eyed god Woten, whom the Norsemen called Odin.

It is Charlemagne above all the warrior-kings of Europe who is generally credited with being the most forceful destroyer of the cult of Odin, and his Germanic equivalent, Woten. Charlemagne's role as 'Defender of the Christian Faith' was considerably more aggressive than that title implies. He made the Rhine his battle line and brutally suppressed all non-Christian worship. He destroyed and pulled down the heathen temples and burned the sacred groves of the pagan religion. All who worshipped Odin/Woten were converted or put to the sword. Similarly to the south, in Spain, he stopped forever the advance of the Saracens. He turned back the tide of Islam and put the worshippers of the prophet Mohammed to the sword.

In *The Lord of the Rings*, Aragorn has a similar subduing effect on all worshippers of Sauron. The Southron and Easterling tribes are forced at sword point to sue for peace. Once the Dark Tower is destroyed, and the Orc legions all but extinguished, the enthralment to Sauron ends among the barbarians. Although there are no religious implications, the barbarians are converted to peaceful ways and sign treaties recognizing the Reunited Kingdom of the Dúnedain.

Naturally, there are many other ways in which Aragorn and Charlemagne are comparable. Both carry magical, ancestral swords, both have the power to cure with magical herbs, both have wise old mentors, and both marry Elf Queens.

Aragorn's sword Andúril – which was forged by Telchar the Smith – is matched by Charlemagne's sword Joyeuse – which was forged by Wayland the Smith. However, it does seem curious that the Christian destroyer of the pagan religions should be armed with a sword that was forged by the same smith who made Gram, the weapon of that supreme warrior of Odin, Sigurd the Dragonslayer.

In *The Lord of the Rings*, Aragorn uses the herb 'athelas' to cure those who are fatally struck down by the 'Black Breath' of the Nazgûl. In the Carolingian Legends, Charlemagne was reputed to have been able to cure those struck down by the plague or 'Black Death' by using the herb called 'sowthistle'. In both cases, these herbs only worked their magical cures if administered by the healing hands of kings – as is acknowledged in the folklore of Middle-earth where the common name for 'athelas' is 'kingsfoil'.

The key figure of Gandalf the Wizard in *The Lord of the Rings*, as Aragorn's mentor and spiritual guide, cannot properly be transferred into Charlemagne's world. The Church would not allow a Wizard as a mentor and spiritual guide to the Holy Roman Emperor. This is especially true as most Wizards are to a great extent thinly veiled, earthbound versions of the pagan magician-god Odin/Woten, the Church's greatest enemy. Consequently, in Charlemagne's Christianized tales, the Gandalf/Merlin/Odin figure is replaced by a wise and elderly churchman. The historical figure of Bishop Turpin supplants the Wizard, and becomes a Christianized version of the same character: the white-bearded, wise old mentor with a bishop's crook instead of a Wizard's staff.

In their choice of queens, Aragorn and Charlemagne are well matched. Aragorn's betrothal to the Elf princess Arwen is comparable to Charlemagne's engagement to the exotic oriental Elf princess Frastrada. Naturally, both Frastrada and Arwen are considered the most beautiful women in the world.

The most compelling of all the Carolingian Ring Legends is the tale that concerns Charlemagne's marriage to Frastrada. Curiously, this story of Charlemagne and 'The Serpent's Ring' is the Carolingian tale that most resembles *The Lord of the Rings* in those elements that relate to the enslaving power of the ring. 'The Serpent's Ring' is also the only ring legend that even comes close to Tolkien's moral stance in the rejection of the ring's power. It is also a tale that demonstrates how a pagan ring still retained sufficient power in the Christian era to overcome even that most devout hero, the Holy Roman Emperor.

The tale of 'The Serpent's Ring' begins on Charlemagne's and Frastrada's royal wedding day. Vassals and peers from all over the world come to the court of Charlemagne with wedding gifts. Among them is a great serpent with a gold ring in its mouth. The serpent enters the banquet hall and creeps onto the royal table. There he raises himself up and drops the gold ring from his mouth into the goblet of the Emperor. The serpent then turns and slithers out of the banquet hall.

Taking this as a good omen on his wedding day, Charlemagne takes up the ring and places it on the hand of his new Queen, Frastrada. However, this serpent ring has a power that Charlemagne has not guessed at; and once on Frastrada's hand that power begins to work.

The Serpent's Ring is a ring of enchantment. Charlemagne's love for Frastrada immediately doubles and redoubles. It becomes a compulsive, almost unbearable thing. By its power Charlemagne is irrevocably bound to love and cherish whoever wears the ring. Never can he bear to be parted from the one who has it upon his or her hand.

For a time, all is well, for Frastrada returns Charlemagne's love and the two are happy and the affairs of the kingdom go well. But after a few years, Frastrada catches a deathly illness, and nothing even the healing hands of Charlemagne can do will save her.

Yet when she dies, the spell of the ring does not abate. She is to be buried in a tomb in the cathedral of Mayence, but Charlemagne refuses to be parted from Frastrada and has her laid out in a chamber where he sits to watch over her body both by day and night. The power of the ring compels him to see her as beautiful as she was in life. So he remains there day after day, week after week, wasting away and neglecting his empire. Finally, Bishop Turpin comes to the chamber while Charlemagne lies in a fitful sleep. Like the wise Gandalf who first recognizes the power of the One Ring, it is the old sage Turpin who recognizes the power of the Serpent's Ring. Wishing to release his Emperor from the ring's spell, Turpin removes it from the Queen's hand and flees from the chamber.

When the Emperor awakens, he finds that, although still saddened by Frastrada's death, the savage grief that enslaved him is magically gone. He no longer feels compelled to remain by her side and permits her body to be entombed.

However, Charlemagne gradually realizes that he must urgently seek the advice and company of Bishop Turpin. He feels that he had neverbefore realized how important this elderly adviser was to him. It seems to him now that only through his friendship with Bishop Turpin can his life have meaning and purpose.

The Emperor immediately rushes to Turpin and declares the Bishop the wisest of men and the best of friends. Thereafter, he proclaims, the Emperor will never be parted from him, and in all affairs of state Turpin's word will hold sway.

Rather daunted by the realization that the power of the ring can arouse such love in Charlemagne for a man as well as for a woman, Turpin nonetheless takes advantage of its powers so that he can get Charlemagne to restore his own health, and then encourages him to attend to the pressing affairs of his realm.

This Turpin manages to achieve, but finally the Bishop decides he must reject the power of the ring. Like the Hobbit Frodo in *The Lord of the Rings*, Turpin discovers that the burden of the ring soon becomes too much. However, the old Bishop mistrusts its sorcerous power and is fearful lest the ring fall into evil hands. He knows that the Emperor will become enslaved and enchanted by anyone who places it on his hand. So, like the Hobbit Frodo, he secretly creeps away into the wilderness and looks for a way of disposing of the ring.

Frodo takes the One Ring to the volcanic fires of Mount Doom in an attempt to neutralize its power. Bishop Turpin finds a remote lake in a forest and throws the ring into its water in his attempt to neutralize its power.

When the Bishop returns to Charlemagne the next morning, he finds to his great relief that the Emperor's infatuation for him has diminished to the simple comradeship of old.

However, that was not an end to the matter. For the serpent's ring was not destroyed by being thrown in the lake any more than the One Ring was destroyed when it was lost in the Anduin River. And as the power of the One Ring called out to Sauron, so the power of the serpent's ring calls out to Charlemagne.

In ways he cannot understand, the ring haunts Charlemagne. His days are restless and his moods will not allow him to concentrate on affairs of state. Full of distraction, he feels compelled to travel and roam distant woodlands. He often calls his huntsmen and wanders the forests of his realm, hoping the chase will dispel his restlessness.

One day Charlemagne enters a particular forest where he feels compelled to go deeper and deeper into its heart, until at last he comes to an open glade wherein he finds that same lake where Turpin had thrown the ring.

Great joy fills Charlemagne at the sight of the crystal pool. Inexplicably he becomes enraptured with the lake in the glade. As he looks on it, his love for this place increases and increases again. He desires nothing so much as to remain in this place all his life.

So it happens that upon this very spot the Emperor commands that a great palace and his new court be built. This was how Aix-la-Chapelle became the capital of Charlemagne's realm, for this was where that glade and pool were found, and there the Emperor spent most of his days.

It is rather startling to find at the symbolic centre of the realm of the premier Christian monarch a magical pagan ring jealously guarded by an emperor armed with a magical pagan sword.

This seems a mirror opposite to the original Norse tale of Andvari's ring where the greedy Dwarf guards a gold ring hidden in a deep pool to keep it from questing heroes. In the Carolingian legend, we have a virtuous emperor guarding a gold ring hidden in a deep pool to keep it from evil pagan powers who come to dethrone him and destroy his empire.

It is also the opposite of the corrupt Gollum in his dark subterranean pool guarding his ring; and an evil emperor like Sauron guarding a gold ring hidden in a Dark Tower to keep it from the good Elvish powers who come to dethrone him and destroy his empire.

Like King Arthur and his Round Table of knights, the Emperor Charlemagne was the focal point of a multitude of tales, known as the 'Chansons de geste', that concern his loyal paladins. Some aspects of these adventures and their heroes appear to find their way into Tolkien's *The Lord of the Rings*.

One of the most famous of Charlemagne's paladins was the hero Roland. Celebrated in that masterpiece of medieval literature, the 'Song of Roland', this loyal paladin is best known for his famous last stand in the Roncevalles Pass in the Pyrenees against the Saracens. Ambushed and vastly outnumbered, Roland fights valiantly on until his sword breaks. Finally he is overwhelmed by the infidel hordes. As he dies, Roland blows his horn to warn Charlemagne of the attack.

In *The Lord of the Rings*, this event is comparable to the last stand of the ranger captain Boromir in his battle with the Orcs on Amon Hen above the Falls of Rauros. Ambushed by Orcs below the Hill of the Eye, Boromir blows his horn. Though he slaughters a score of Orcs in defence of the Hobbits, he is overwhelmed. His sword is broken and his great horn smashed. Aragorn, like Charlemagne, rushes to the sound of the horn but, like Charlemagne, he reaches his valiant friend too late. Boromir speaks only a few words before he dies.

Another of Charlemagne's great paladins was the hero whom the Danes praise above all other Christian knights. This was Ogier the Dane. The son of King Geoffrey of Denmark, Ogier's deeds were celebrated in the 'Chansons de geste' and many other legend cycles. In the nineteenth century, William Morris wrote of Ogier the Dane in his book-length poem, 'The Earthly Paradise'. As Holger Danske, Ogier is today still the national hero of Denmark.

Ogier the Dane was numbered among the greatest knights of the world. He knew the courts of Charlemagne, of Arthur, of the Langobards, the Huns and Saracens, and embarked on adventures that took him to Jerusalem and Babylon. In his hundredth year, Ogier embarked on one last quest on his return from Jerusalem. He travelled to an isle where a great castle was made of lodestone that tore all iron from ships that attempted to sail near its shores. Ogier's ship was wrecked, but he made his way to shore. The castle was illuminated by a magical light and Ogier entered it. There he discovered a great serpent in its central court who guarded a tree in the garden. Ogier drew his sword Courtain and slew the creature. Beneath the tree was the most beautiful woman Ogier had ever seen, and on her hand was a gold ring.

The maid was none other than the immortal Morgan the Fay, the faerie sister of King Arthur. When Morgan placed the golden ring on the old warrior's hand, Ogier's youth was instantly restored. By its power, Ogier was granted eternal youth and immortal life. Young and golden-haired once more, Ogier and Morgan went on a final voyage across the sea to the distant faerie realm of Avalon.

In this Carolingian ring legend, we find many elements comparable to Tolkien's tales. We have a hero on a ring quest who slays a dragon with an ancestral sword. With the ring he wins his Elf princess and immortal life as they sail in a faerie ship to a blessed isle of immortals across the sea. Most importantly, however, in Ogier and Morgan, we have the pattern of Aragorn and Arwen: the marriage of the mortal prince and the immortal princess who make a choice between mortal and immortal worlds. Ogier and Morgan choose the immortal world; while Aragorn and Arwen choose the mortal one.

CHAPTER EIGHT

CELTIC AND SAXON MYTHS

In looking for sources for and influences on the imagination of J. R. R. Tolkien, one must eventually come to the mythologies of the two great races from whom the British people are largely descended: the Celts and the Anglo-Saxons. As a professor of Anglo-Saxon, Tolkien had a great love for the heroic story-telling traditions of this bold warrior race with their wonderful sagas, chronicles and adventure tales. He was also vividly aware that these rough Teutonic warriors supplanted the older, more sophisticated Celtic civilization and its fluid language and poetry.

In looking at Arthurian legends, we could see the strong influence of the Celtic traditions that filtered through to Tolkien's tales. Besides those elements already mentioned, Celtic mythology has played a fundamental part in the shaping of Tolkien's world. When we learn that the most important source of Welsh Celtic lore was preserved in the fourteenth-century *Red Book of Hergest*, we realize that Tolkien is making a small scholarly joke in naming his 'source' of Elf-lore the *Red Book of Westmarch*.

The *Red Book of Hergest* is a manuscript that includes that most important compendium of Welsh legends, 'The Mabinogion'. That collection contains many stories of magic rings. The damsel Luned, the Lady of the Fountain, gives a Ring of Invisibility to the hero Owain. Dame Lyonesse gives her hero Gareth a magical ring that will not allow him to be wounded. And Percival Long Spear goes on a quest for a gold ring during which he slays the Black Serpent of the Barrows and wins a stone of invisibility and a gold-making stone.

However, the most important aspect of the Celtic influence on Tolkien's imagination relates to how much its mythology contributed to the creation of his 'Elves'. In general terms, it is quite easy to see that Tolkien has largely aligned the traditions of the older Celtic peoples with his Elves; while the invading race of Anglo-Saxons have the characteristics of his Men.

Tolkien's Elves are largely based on the traditions and conventions of the Celtic myths and legends of Ireland and Wales. However, it is important to understand that before Tolkien the 'Elf' was a vaguely defined concept associated most often with pixies, flower-fairies, gnomes, dwarfs, and goblins of a diminutive and inconsequential nature.

Tolkien's Elves are not a race of pixies. They are a powerful, full-blooded people who closely resemble the pre-human Irish race of immortals called the Tuatha Dé Danann. Like the Tuatha Dé Danann, Tolkien's Elves are taller and stronger than mortals, are incapable of suffering sickness, are possessed of more than human beauty, and are filled with greater wisdom in all things. They possess talismans, jewels and weapons that humans might consider magical in their powers. They ride supernatural horses and understand the languages of animals. They love song, poetry and music – all of which they compose and perform perfectly.

The Tuatha Dé Danann gradually withdrew from Ireland as mortal men migrated there from the east. With his ever-present theme of the dwindling of Elvish power on Middle-earth, Tolkien was following the tradition of Celtic myth. The Elves' westward sailings to timeless immortal realms across the sea, while the human race remained behind and usurped a mortal, diminished world trapped in time, were very much the theme of the diminishing of the Tuatha Dé Danann.

The remnant of this once mighty race was the 'Aes Sídhe' or the 'Sídhe' (pronounced 'Shee'). The name means the 'people of the hills', for it was believed that these people withdrew from the mortal realm and hid themselves inside the 'hollow hills' or within ancient mounds once sacred to them. In Tolkien, as in Celtic legends, we have remnant populations of these immortals in all manner of hiding-places: enchanted woods (like Lothlórien), hidden valleys (like Rivendell), in caves (like Menegroth), in river gorges (like Nargothrond), and on distant islands (like Tol Eressëa). Tolkien's Elves, like the Sídhe, seldom intrude on the world of men. They are far more concerned with their own affairs and histories. The Celtic traditions of the Sídhe are all to be found in Tolkien's Elves. Elven time is very different from mortal time; when Tolkien's mortal adventurers pass through an Elven realm they experience a jolt in time, not unlike that of mortals held within their realms by the Sídhe – in

extreme cases, sometimes mistaking hours for years, or years for hours. This may be due to the rules of immortality by which both the Elves and the Sídhe are governed.

Both the Elves and the Sídhe are immortal in the same sense that their lifespan is unlimited, but they can be killed. Tolkien follows the Celtic tradition that suggests that immortals cannot survive in a mortal world; that they can remain only at the cost of their powers diminishing. Ultimately, there is a choice between remaining in the mortal world and leaving it forever for another immortal timeless world beyond the reach of human understanding.

Although Tolkien used elements of Celtic myth in his creation of his Elvish race, his original contribution to these creatures of his imagination is immense and remarkable. Tolkien took the sketchy myths and legends of the Sídhe and the Tuatha Dé Danann and created a vast civilization, history and genealogy for his Elves. He gave them languages and a vast cultural inheritance rooted in real history but flourishing in his imagination.

There are some curious comparisons as well. In *The Lord of the Rings* we have Sauron the Evil Eye, the lord and master of the Orcs, Trolls, Balrogs and most other monstrous beings. In Celtic myth, we have Balor the Evil Eye, the king of the monstrous race of deformed giants called the Formors who were the chief rivals of the Tuatha Dé Danann for the land of Ireland before the coming of men.

The hideous Balor had two eyes: one was normal, but the other was huge and swollen. He kept the huge eye shut because it had been filled with such horrific, sorcerous powers that it virtually incinerated whoever and whatever it looked upon. In war, Balor was brought into the battlefield like a piece of artillery. He took his place in the Formor front line facing his enemies while a henchman used a hook to lift his eyelid and his comrades looked away. In Balor's case, looks could kill, and any who were within the blaze of his fiery eye were instantly destroyed.

Many fell to King Balor's Eye until the coming of the champion of the Tuatha Dé Danann, the golden-haired warrior Lugh of the Long Arm. Seeing the blaze of light just as Balor's eyelid was being lifted by the hook, the god shot a stone with his rod-sling straight into the fiery Eye. His stone was hurled with such force that the Evil Eye was driven right through the back of Balor's skull into the ranks of the Formor army ranged behind the king. There the blazing Eye incinerated half Balor's own monstrous army and the Formors were driven from the field.

There were other Celtic characters who appear to have found their way to Middle-earth. Tolkien's Valarian god, Oromë the Huntsman, was called Araw in the Sindarin language of the Elves. Almost identical in both name and character is the Welsh god Arawn the Huntsman. Both have an immortal giant horse and a pack of supernatural hounds.

In Celtic legend we often find the mystical appearance of a 'lady in white', and in Arthurian romances such figures as the Lady of the Lake and Morgan the Fay. In Tolkien we have the Elf Queen Galadriel (whose name means 'lady of light' and who is sometimes called 'the White Lady'), and the archetype of them all: Varda, the Queen of the Stars. Varda is the goddess most loved by the Elves, and a Valarian version of Galadriel. In these figures we see that Tolkien adopts the convention of the link between Elves and starlight, which is a constant feature of the Celtic Sídhe. The Sídhe similarly love to walk beneath the starlit sky. Like Tolkien's Elves they are also generally perceived by mortals as having eyes like stars, and bodies that shimmer with light.

In the Celtic tradition, when these radiant beings – these 'ladies in white'– take on mortal heroes as lovers, there are always obstacles to overcome. These obstacles usually take the form of an almost impossible quest. This is most clearly comparable to Tolkien in the Welsh legend of the wooing of Olwyn. Olwyn was the most beautiful woman of her age; her eyes shone with light, and her skin was white as snow. Olwyn's name means 'she of the white track', so bestowed because four white trefoils sprang up with her every step on the forest floor, and the winning of her hand required the near-impossible gathering of the 'Treasures of Britain'.

In Tolkien, we have two almost identical 'ladies in white': Lúthien in *The Silmarillion*, and Arwen in *The Lord of the Rings*. Both these Elf princesses are considered the most beautiful women of their time; both have eyes that shine with light, and skin as white as snow. Both are connected with a white star-shaped flower called Niphredil. This is a flower that first bloomed in celebration of Lúthien's birth, and blossomed eternally on both Lúthien and Arwen's burial mounds. And finally, the winning of both required near-impossible quests. For the mortal hero Beren to win Lúthien, the Silmaril had to be captured; and for the mortal hero Aragorn to win Arwen, the One Ring had be destroyed.

The degree to which Tolkien's Elves were inspired by Celtic models is most obviously demonstrated by looking at his invented Elvish language, Sindarin. Tolkien himself noted that his invented language and Elvish names of persons and places were 'mainly deliberately modelled on those of Welsh (closely similar but not identical).' Structurally and phonetically, there are strong links between the two languages.*

Although the Celts were the older civilization in Britain, it was the Anglo-Saxons who were the dominant race from whom the British inherited most of their language and consequently most of their culture. Tolkien being a professor of Anglo-Saxon, we can see how his expertise in this area influenced his imagination in relation to aspects of his human cultures, as much as that of the Celts influenced his Elves. It must also be remembered that Tolkien frequently expressed his desire to restore the mythology and literature of early England to the English. By this he meant the lost mythology and literature of Anglo-Saxon Britain between the time of the Roman retreat in AD 419 and the Norman Conquest in AD 1066. With the notable exception of 'Beowulf' and a handful of poem fragments, the ruthless obliteration of Anglo-Saxon culture by the Norman conquerors was nearly absolute.

In his imaginative writing, Tolkien wished to retrieve something of the atmosphere of that lost age of heroes and dragons. Consequently, we see Anglo-Saxon elements playing a critical part in his writing. His mortals predominantly speak Westron or the Common Speech of Men which is 'translated' as modern English; however, many of the names and places relating to Men are 'translated' as Anglo-Saxon – or Old English. Hundreds of Old English words are employed. Indeed, we find all the Northmen and Rohirrim names (like 'Éowyn' – 'horsewoman', and

*A few words are identical: 'mal' means 'gold' in both the Welsh and Sindar tongues. Others are close: 'du' means 'black' in Welsh and 'shadow' in Sindarin; 'calan' means 'first day' in Welsh and 'daylight' in Sindarin; 'ost' means 'host' in Welsh and 'town' in Sindarin; 'sarn' in Welsh means a stone 'causeway' and in Sindarin means a 'stone' in a ford. There are many others close in spelling and/or meaning: 'fortress' is 'caer' in Welsh and 'caras' in Sindarin; 'drud' in Welsh means 'fierce' while 'dru' in Sindarin means 'wild'; 'dagr' in Welsh means 'dagger' while 'dagor' in Sindarin means 'battle'. Others are the same words with different meanings: 'adan' is 'birds' in Welsh and 'man' in Sindarin; 'nen' is 'heaven' in Welsh and 'water' in Sindarin; 'nar' is 'lord' in Welsh and 'sun' in Sindarin. Some others are strangely connected: 'iar' in Sindarin means 'old', while the Welsh 'iar' means 'hen'; however, the Welsh word 'hen' actually means 'old'. Coincidentally, a few of Tolkien's characters take their names directly from Welsh words: 'Morwen' means 'maid'; 'Bard' means 'poet'; 'Barahir' means 'longbeard'.

'Théoden' – 'chief of a nation') are in Old English – as the names of the Dwarves are Icelandic, and those of the Elves are rooted in Welsh.

Also, the names Men give to other races are often rooted in Old English. Ent is Old English for giant, Orc is demon or goblin, Meara is horse, Hobbit is from invented Old English 'Holbytla' or 'hole builder'. Woses is from 'wodwos', a sylvan goblin. Púkel Men is from 'puckle' meaning goblin or demon, which Shakespeare translated into his character Puck.

In the Teutonic hero cycles popular among the Anglo-Saxons we can see some elements that undoubtedly influenced Tolkien's writing. This was particularly true in ring-related tales.

The importance of the Volsung ring legend in establishing royal lineage and historic stature can be easily recognized in history and literature throughout northern Europe. Even in the oldest surviving Teutonic epic, that eighth-century masterpiece of Anglo-Saxon literature, 'Beowulf', the ring legend and its hero Sigurd are discernible.

There is no doubt that the tale of Beowulf was an Anglo-Saxon attempt to rival the greatness of the Volsung hero. Before the scald sings his tribute to Beowulf, he begins by singing first of Sigurd. Calling him Siegmund in the Anglo-Saxon version, he is said to be the most famous of all heroes whose greatest of many deeds was the slaying of a dragon and the winning of a ring-hoard. The scald gives such an abbreviated version of the legend, it is obvious that this is an allusion to a legend that everyone is familiar with. Furthermore, it is used to foreshadow Beowulf's dragon battle which will win him comparable fame among his own folk.

When Beowulf slays the monster Grendel, he is rewarded with gold finger rings, arm rings and neck rings by King Hrothgar, 'Lord of the Ring-Danes'. Decades later, Beowulf rules as the Lord of the Ring-Danes in Hrothgar's place, and his last heroic deed is to do battle with a terrible flying fire-breathing dragon that is guardian of a huge ring-hoard of an ancient vanished race.

Tolkien, as a professor of Anglo-Saxon, was an authority on Beowulf, and has acknowledged that 'Beowulf is among my most valued sources' for his Hobbit tale. The two tales are not very obviously similar; however, there are strong parallels in the plot structure of the dragon episode of Beowulf and that of the slaying of Smaug in *The Hobbit*. Beowulf's dragon is awakened by a thief who finds his way into the dragon's cavern and steals a jewelled cup from the treasure hoard. This is duplicated by Bilbo Baggins' burglary in Smaug the Dragon's cavern, when the Hobbit also steals a jewelled cup from the treasure hoard. Both thieves escape detection and the anger of the dragons themselves; however, the nearby human settlements in both tales suffer terribly from the dragon's wrath.

It is up to their respective champions, Beowulf and Bard the Bowman, to slay the beast. This they both do, although Bard survives to become King of Dale, while Beowulf does not. Following the pattern of Sigmund in his last battle, Beowulf's sword 'Nailing' breaks, and although he is victorious, he dies of his wounds. Beowulf's death is mirrored in *The Hobbit*, not by Bard, but by that other warrior-king of the tale, the Dwarf Thorin Oakenshield, who lives long enough to know that he has been victorious, but dies of his wounds on the battlefield.

Tolkien also used elements of Beowulf in *The Lord of the Rings*. To begin with, the Hobbit hero Frodo (which we are told in original Hobbitish is actually Froda) is named after a character in Beowulf: Froda, lord of the Bards. Also, in his creation of the golden-haired Horsemen of Rohan, and in particular his description of the Golden Hall of Meduseld (Old English for 'mead hall'), we see elements of Beowulf's world. This gold-roofed feast hall of King Théoden is very much modelled on Herot, the hall of King Hrothgar in 'Beowulf', with its roof gables covered with hammered gold which shone in the sun from afar – just as Meduseld was perceived in the distance. And both these earthly halls were mortal versions of the god Odin's titanic gold-roofed hall Valhalla.

Other Anglo-Saxon tales also made major contributions to Tolkien's writings. One certainly was the ring legend of the Saxon hero Wayland the Smith. Wayland's tales were extremely popular during the Middle Ages. He was a Saxon Daedalus, and the greatest craftsman of his race. Again it was a legend with which Tolkien was familiar. Humphrey Carpenter, in his biography of Tolkien, notes that during the period in which he was writing *The Lord of the Rings*, Tolkien took his family on a holiday outing to White Horse Hill, less than twenty miles from Oxford on the borders of Mercia and Wessex. This is the site of the famous image of the White Horse cut in chalk on the green hill which gave Tolkien the image for his Riders of Mark banner: 'a white horse on a green field'. Just beyond this hill, the family went on to see the ancient long-barrow known as Wayland's Smithy.

In the Middle Ages, it became traditional for the swords of great heroes to come from the forge of Wayland the Smith. In the Nibelungenlied, Siegfried's sword Balmung was of Wayland's making; as was Charlemagne's blade Joyeuse. In the Wilkina Saga, Wayland forges the sword Mimung or Mimming for his heroic son Witig, but the blade also makes its way to the hero, Dietrich von Berne. Wayland is also the sword-maker in the Waltharius, for the Saxon hero Walter of Aquitaine.

Most remarkable of all, one Wayland tale claims that after fleeing to the realm of the Elf-smiths of Alfheim, the hero-smith gave his own sword to Odin the Allfather. This was the same sword that Odin takes to Midgard and drives into the tree Branstock: Gram, the fiery sword of the Volsunga Saga.

In Wayland the Smith we have the figure of the gifted but cursed smith who in Tolkien is manifest in Noldor King Fëanor, who made the Silmarils that were stolen by Morgoth. He is also comparable to Telchar the Smith, the supreme

Dwarf-smith who forged the Dúnedain sword inherited by Aragorn with which Elendil cuts the One Ring from Sauron's hand. Telchar also forged the dagger 'Angrist' which Beren used in the Quest of the Silmaril to cut the jewel from Morgoth's iron crown. More particularly, however, we can see in the tale of Wayland's Ring something of the figure of Celebrimbor, Lord of the Elven-smiths of Eregion, who forged the Rings of Power.

The tale of the Ring of Wayland the Smith – known as Weiland to the Germans – comes to us largely through a later Norse version, in which the Saxon hero is called Völund. This was written down in the long Icelandic narrative poem, the Völundarkvitha.

The tale of Völund begins with his winning of a Valkyrie wife, who had descended to earth in the guise of a swan maiden. Völund captures the plumage of this swan maid, thus preventing her escape, and in her form as a mortal woman he takes her as a wife. After nine years the Valkyrie discovers the hiding-place of her plumage and flees the mortal world. However, as a token of her continued love for him, she leaves Völund a magical ring of the purest gold.

By the powers of this ring, Völund's already formidable skills increase beyond that of all men. Weapons and armour blessed with fantastic powers, and jewels of exquisite beauty and intricacy, come forth from Völund's forge. Most valued of Völund's creations are his swords, the best of all being his own sword which always has fire playing around its razor edge. It is a blade that can never be blunted or broken, and any who hold it cannot be defeated in battle.

Völund's ring is also a source of almost infinite wealth. Placing his ring upon his forge, Völund pounds out with his hammer seven hundred gold rings of equal weight from its shape. So great is Völund's wealth that Nidud, the King of Sweden, sends his soldiers to capture the smith and seize his treasures and his magical ring.

The evil king then makes a slave of Völund. He has the smith crippled by hamstringing him, then exiled to a rocky isle where he is forced to build a fortress labyrinth that serves as his own prison. Here Völund is ordered to make jewels, ornaments and weapons for his master's amusement.

After many years, Völund manages by trickery to avenge himself on Nidud by slaying the king's sons, violating his daughter and regaining his sword and his ring. Völund then uses his skills to forge a pair of huge wings, much like those of the Valkyrie swan maiden who was once his wife.

With these wings, he flies out of his island prison and far beyond Midgard and the realm of mortal men. He flies to that place called Alfheim, the land of the Elfs, where live the finest smiths in creation. But so great is Völund's skill that the Elf-smiths welcome him as a peer. With the Elfs of Alfheim and the power of the ring, Völund conceives and fashions many a miraculous work for gods and heroes, greater than any he made in the world of men.

In some lost version of the legends, Völund's ring appears to have been stolen in Alfheim by the Dwarf Andvari and taken back into Midgard. There it becomes Andvarinaut, the self-same ring of the Volsunga Saga.

However, in the surviving versions of the Völund tale, his ring has another destiny. It does not remain in Alfheim but is stolen by a daring mortal pirate called Soté the Outlaw. After taking the ring, he becomes obsessed with it. Fearful that someone will steal it from him, he flees to Bretland and has himself buried alive in a hollow barrow grave. In this great mound, with drawn sword and dagger, he wanders the passages, never sleeping, awaiting any who might attempt to take the fabulous ring. Soté the Outlaw becomes a haunted, blasted spirit. Possessed and cursed by the power of the ring, Soté becomes an immortal ring-wraith, one of the living-dead that men called barrow-wights, who haunts the graves of men.

Völund's Ring is the object of the quest of hero Thorsten. When Thorsten comes at last to Bretland, he enters the hollow hill that was the barrow grave where Soté the Outlaw hid. The wailing screams of a tortured fiend, the cries of a living man, and the sound of steel striking stone and bone are heard, and the flickering of sorcerous flames can be seen within. Finally Thorsten emerges from the dark passage, pale and bloody as a ghost himself, but in his left hand is the glinting gold of Völund's Ring.

The latter part of the tale of Völund's Ring is certainly a major source for Tolkien for his Hobbits' near-fatal encounter with the barrow-wights of the Barrow Downs. Of course, the difference is that although the barrow-wights had their own treasures, it was Frodo who possessed the Ring. Also in Tolkien's tale, it is that odd creation Tom Bombadil who bursts into the barrow grave to scatter the barrow-wights and save the Ringbearer and his companions.

However, with the introduction of the barrow-wight spirit – in the figure of Soté the Outlaw – we see the concept of a ring that gives mortals immortality and fiendish powers but which also enslaves them and destroys their human souls. Perhaps in Soté the Outlaw there is something of the Witch-king and the Ringwraiths of *The Lord of the Rings* – mortal men who become immortal, blasted spirits through the rings of power.

In Soté's paranoid, ghoulish behaviour after he steals the ring, we may also perceive something of the character of Sméagol Gollum. For after Gollum murders his cousin and steals the One Ring, like Soté he becomes obsessed with this 'precious' ring and in a kind of miserly madness he also buries himself alive. In the foul tunnels of an abandoned Orc hold beneath the hills, Gollum hides (like Soté) and murders any who dare to come near, for fear that they might steal his precious ring.

CHAPTER NINE

GERMAN ROMANCE

The medieval German legend that most resembles the imaginative sweep and dramatic impact of *The Lord of the Rings* is the tale of the hero Dietrich von Berne and Virginal the Ice Queen of Jeraspunt. There are aspects of this tale that are suggestive of the major themes and characters in both *The Lord of the Rings* and *The Silmarillion*.

Of all the heroes of medieval German romance, Dietrich von Berne is certainly the greatest. This mighty Ostrogoth hero who was also called Dietrich of Verona was, like Arthur and Charlemagne, a central figure around which a large number of hero cycles were told. Also like Charlemagne, Dietrich was based on a real historical figure: in this case, Theodoric the Goth, who eventually became Theodoric the Great, the sixth-century (454–526) Roman Emperor.

From Tolkien's letters, we know that he was fascinated with the Goths. As a student, he stumbled on a book of Gothic grammar that 'took him by storm'. He felt that surviving fragments of Gothic text combined with reading of Latin historical documents gave him exciting insights into an authentic ancient German culture. And although he was more interested in the historical Theodoric the Goth, he was obviously imaginatively provoked by the adventures of the romantic Dietrich von Berne.

The tale of Dietrich and the Ice Queen begins with the hero entering the realm of a race of Mountain Giants ruled over by Orkis the cannibal Giant, and his evil son, Janibas the Wizard. Dietrich learns that the Giants were making war on the highest mountain kingdom of the Ice Faeries in the snow-peaked Alps. This was the domain of the magical snow maidens who were ruled by Virginal, the Ice Queen, from her glittering Castle of Jeraspunt, on the highest peak in the Alps.

Dietrich carries out a long campaign of war on the Mountain Giants, slaying one after the other and taking mountain castle after mountain castle. In one titanic battle, he meets and kills the terrible Giant Orkis himself. However, when he arrives within sight of the Ice Castle, he finds the way barred by the son of the Giant King – a foe more formidable than Orkis himself. For Janibas the Wizard has laid siege to the shining castle with an awesome army of Giants, evil men, and monsters. To his foes, Janibas appears as a phantom Black Rider who commands tempests and is backed by demons and hell-hounds. But the Wizard's most terrifying power is his ability to command those who were slain in battle to rise up from the dead and fight again.

Beyond his ambition to seize the realm of the Ice Queen and the Ice Castle, Janibas' main driving desire is to enhance his sorcerer's powers by taking possession of the magical jewel in the crown of the Ice Queen. For by the powers of this jewel she can command the elements of the lands of ice and snow, and by it she rules the mountains.

Dietrich can see the siege

army lying like a black sea around the many-towered Ice Castle. It is obvious that, however well defended, the Castle must eventually fall to the never-dwindling numbers of the sorcerer's army. Despite what would seem an impossible task, Dietrich is spurred to a battle frenzy by the sight of the beautiful Ice Queen on the battlements of the tallest tower. Her radiance matches even that of the star-like jewel dancing in her crown with icy light.

In his valiant attempt to raise the siege Dietrich slaughters all before him, but this proves futile as the dead simply rise up to fight again. Dietrich then decides on another strategy. Seeing that Janibas commands his forces by means of a sorcerer's iron tablet held aloft, Dietrich pursues the Black Horseman himself. Striking Janibas down from his phantom steed, Dietrich lifts his sword and smashes the iron tablet. As the tablet breaks, the glaciers of the mountains split and shatter, thundering down in massive avalanches that bury the whole evil host of Giants and phantoms and undead forever.

Dietrich triumphantly makes his way to the Castle as the gates are flung open to greet him. He is welcomed by the incomparable Ice Queen herself, surrounded by her dazzling court of snow maidens, all aglow with fairy light and the glitter of diamond veils. Here in the Ice Castle of Jeraspunt, in the realm of the Ice Faeries, Dietrich and the Ice Queen are wed.

In the legend of the Ice Queen, Janibas the Necromancer as the Black Horseman is very like a combination of Sauron the Necromancer and his chief lieutenant, the Witch-king lord of the Ringwraiths. The One Ring is replaced by an iron tablet, but the climax of the tale reads very like Sauron's ultimate battle at the Black Gate at the end of *The Lord of the Rings*. The result of the destruction of the iron tablet on Janibas' evil legions is identical to the destruction of the One Ring on those of Sauron.

Janibas' father Orkis, the King of the Mountain Giants, is very like Sauron's ancient master, Morgoth the Dark Enemy, who ruled the evil mountain realm of Angband in *The Silmarillion*. It is interesting to note that the cause of Morgoth's war with the Elves is the star-like Silmaril jewels that Morgoth wears in his Iron Crown. The cause of Orkis's war with the Faeries is the star-like jewel that the Ice Queen wears in her crown.

Although the Ice Queen is comparable to the Elf Queen Galadriel in her enchanted forest realm of Lothlórien, or even the Elf Princess Arwen in Imladris in *The Lord of the Rings*, the siege of the Ice Faerie Castle of Jeraspunt in the middle of the Alps is more like the many-towered Elven city of Gondolin in the middle of the Encircling Mountains in *The Silmarillion*.

Although in the tale of Dietrich and the Ice Queen aspects of the ring are taken on by the iron tablet and the star-like jewel, there are many legends of German romance where the ring is overtly the key element. This is certainly true of the Langobard and the Amelung hero cycles.

The fierce Langobards were one of the many powerful Germanic tribes who invaded the eastern European borderlands of the Roman Empire. These warrior people later swept into northern Italy where they were known as the Lombards and gave their name to the region today called Lombardy. Described by Latin historians as the supreme horsemen of the Germanic peoples, the Langobards were Tolkien's models for the Rohirrim. Historical accounts of the Langobard cavalry in battle closely resemble the dramatic 'Charge of the Rohirrim' in *The Lord of the Rings*. The hero of the Langobard cycle is Ortnit, who is given a gold ring by his mother that gives him the strength of twelve men. This ring allows him to subdue an innocent-looking, unarmed child blessed with huge physical strength who has slain scores of knights. Once Ortnit makes this rather embarrassing conquest, it is revealed to him that the child is actually none other than the powerful Dwarf King Alberich (the German name for Andvari). He acknowledges that he is the same Dwarf of legend and is now more than five hundred years old. Furthermore, the Dwarf King reveals that the ring on Ortnit's hand once belonged to him, but he gave it to Ortnit's mother as a token of love, for in truth Alberich was Ortnit's true father.

The Dwarf King now joyfully gives his son armour and a sword. The sword, called Rosen, and the armour were both forged by Alberich and tempered in dragon's blood. The sword is unbreakable and the armour is impenetrable. He also tells him that the ring will not only increase his strength, but can also be used to heal the sick and wounded, and can be used magically to summon Alberich himself. With the sword, the armour and the ring, Ortnit wins fame and riches and becomes King of Lombardy. In the end, however, Ortnit meets his end when two dragons crush him to death. His sword and armour remain in their cavern, but his ring is retained by Alberich, until the coming of a hero who might be a worthy heir to Ortnit.

The heir to the ring emerged in the Amelung hero cycle. The Amelungs were a German tribe who rose to prominence when their warrior-king Anzius was crowned Emperor of the Eastern Empire in Constantinople. The greatest hero of the Amelung cycle is Wolfdietrich, who is the rightful heir to the Emperor. However, abandoned in childhood by his brothers, he is raised by wolves. After many adventures, Wolfdietrich comes to Lombardy where he is challenged by the Dwarf Alberich. Winning a test of strength with Alberich, he is awarded Ortnit's ring and goes on to fight the two Dragons of Lombardy. Taking the sword Rosen from Ortnit's dead hand within the cave, Wolfdietrich slays the

Dragons. The victorious Wolfdietrich is married to Ortnit's widow and becomes King of Lombardy. Armed with the ring, sword and armour, Wolfdietrich raises an army, marches on Constantinople and lays claim to his birthright. He is crowned Emperor of the Eastern Empire, but his destiny is not yet fulfilled. He returns to Lombardy with an even greater army, then marches south to Rome where he is crowned Emperor of the West as well. Once again, the master of the ring reunites the ancient broken empire.

In the many German hero cycles, the most persistent character in the ring quest tradition is the guardian of the ring and the treasure. This is the Dwarf known as Andvari in Norse tales, and Alberich in German legends. Although capable of being tamed, he is usually a sinister figure; however, in later romances his appearance and powers often change. He often lends help to other heroes under alternative names: Alferich, Laurin and Elbeghast. Increasingly, this character supplies all the supernatural elements in German romance: dwarf, wizard, elf, smith, guardian and god. By the sixteenth and seventeenth centuries, he is entirely transformed. In Britain, he becomes Auberon, and by Shakespeare's time is the remarkable Oberon, the King of the Faeries. In this role in *A Midsummer Night's Dream*, he is said to be the radiant god of love, and the immortal son of Julius Caesar and Morgan the Fay. Quite a remarkable evolution from a rather nasty Norse Dwarf.

In Tolkien, the Dwarves are often hoarders and guardians of various treasures. However, his equivalent figure to the Dwarf Andvari/Alberich in *The Lord of the Rings* is manifest in the strange character of Sméagol Gollum, the former Hobbit, turned into a tormented ghoul by the curse of the One Ring. He is not far off becoming a Ringwraith enslaved by the power of the One Ring, but manages in some perverse Hobbitish way to remain his own creature.

In medieval German romance, the same Dwarf of the Langobard cycle of Ortnit and the Amelung cycle of Wolfdietrich reappears in the hero cycles of the Goths. Inevitably, their hero Dietrich von Berne encounters Alberich. Legend dictates that Dietrich von Berne was the great-grandson of the Amelung hero, Wolfdietrich. Dietrich goes into battle with the Dwarf King Alberich, who in this particular manifestation rules a subterranean kingdom in the Tyrolean mountains. After various intrigues and battles, Dietrich overthrows the Dwarf and wins his magical golden ring, a girdle of strength, a cape of invisibility, a vast golden treasure, and the sword Nagelring.

Dietrich's exploits as the premier German hero are as extensive as Arthur's and Charlemagne's. His adventures cross over many other ring quest cycles in many rather unexpected ways. Inevitably, the peripatetic Dietrich makes an appearance in the German people's greatest medieval epic, the Nibelungenlied.

As a liegeman to the Hun Emperor Etzel, he is reluctantly drawn into the Nibelung tragedy. He becomes the *deus ex machina* of the epic tale and is forced into a position where he must destroy the last vestige of the Nibelung dynasty.

Although many of the German romances of hero cycles used elements of the Norse Volsunga Saga, the medieval epic the Nibelungenlied is the most direct rendering of that particular tale. Its hero Siegfried is definitely the Norse Sigurd the Dragonslayer. In part, the Nibelungenlied is an attempt by German royal houses to claim mythic ancestors in established heroic tradition; and in part it is authentic history.

The heroic age for all the Teutonic (Germanic and Scandinavian) races of northern Europe was the chaotic fifth and sixth centuries, when the authority of the Roman Empire was collapsing before the migrating Teuton tribes. The historical chieftains of those times became the subjects of oral traditions that elevated them to mythic status. The events in the Volsunga Saga and the Nibelungenlied are both based on the historical events surrounding the catastrophic annihilation of the Burgundians in AD 436 by the Huns of Attila, who were acting as mercenary agents for the Roman Emperor.

The Nibelungenlied, as we know it, was written by an anonymous poet around AD 1200 for performance in the Austrian court – or rather, he was the last poet to contribute to the Nibelungenlied, for the work was the product of a heroic poetic tradition that began sometime in the fifth century.

The Nibelungenlied legend concerns itself with an early Germanic people called the Burgundians who early in the fifth century settled on the Rhine near Worms, which at the time was Roman territory. In the year 436 they arose in rebellion against the Roman governor Aetius. By 437 they had been all but exterminated by a contingent of Huns acting on behalf of the Empire. What remained of the annihilated Burgundians fled the Rhinelands westward and settled on the Rhône, roughly in that part of France now called Burgundy. The memory of this catastrophic end to a once powerful German tribe was recalled vividly by the neighbouring Franks on the Rhine around Cologne. The story was adapted by their Norse neighbours and integrated into the Volsung legend, then – centuries later – was readapted and reclaimed by medieval Germans in the epic tale of the Nibelungenlied.

Although Attila was certainly the Hun King at the time of the Burgundian uprising, he did not participate in its quelling and was elsewhere at the time. However, as the legend grew, inevitably he became part of the tale. (He is the Norse Atli, and the German Etzel.) The source of the Volsung Hun King Atli's death at the hands of his wife is undoubtedly related to the historical events

surrounding Attila's death in the year 453.

Reliable historical accounts tell us that Attila died of a throat haemorrhage after drinking and feasting on the first night of his marriage to a German princess called Hildico. Immediately there sprang up a belief that Hildico had killed Attila in revenge for the Burgundian massacre.

The names of the two great queens of the Nibelungenlied are in fact etymologically connected with this historical German princess. Hildico means 'Little Warrior Maid'; which is fairly close to both Kriemhild, 'Helmed Warrior Maid', and Brunhild, 'Armoured Warrior Maid'.

The characters of Brunhild and Kriemhild – and much of the plot for the Nibelungenlied and the Volsunga Saga – are also partly shaped by another historical character: the notorious Visigoth Queen Brunhilda. Born in about AD 540, Brunhilda was married to King Sigebert of the Eastern Franks. King Sigebert's brother Chilperic was the King of the Western Franks and married Queen Brunhilda's sister. In the ensuing war between brothers, King Sigebert was murdered through intrigue in 575, and Brunhilda was made a captive. Her life was saved and her freedom won, however, by her captor's son, who took her as his wife. She soon became a powerful force among the Franks, and over the thirty years of her influence she brought about the murders of no less than ten royal noblemen. Finally, in 613, a group of Frank noblemen decided to put an end to her intrigues. They tortured Brunhilda for three days, had her torn apart by wild horses, and then burned her on a pyre – a spectacular and barbaric end to a remarkable historical character.

In *The Lord of the Rings*, the basic central plot of the Nibelungenlied can be found in an understated sub-plot involving the four-way romance of Aragorn-Arwen-Éowyn-Faramir. The shield maiden Princess Éowyn of Rohan falls in love with Aragorn in the same hopeless way as it is implied the Amazon warrior Queen Brunhild of Iceland falls for Siegfried. Siegfried is betrothed to the beautiful Kriemhild, in the same way that Aragorn is betrothed to beautiful Arwen of Rivendell. Tolkien's resolution of the love triangle in *The Lord of the Rings* is far happier and more gentlemanly, with none of the low trickery or bloody retribution of the Nibelungenlied.

The Nibelungenlied displays many perspectives that sound strange to a modern reader. The Nibelungenlied epic is not primarily a vehicle for the hero Siegfried, as, say, the Iliad is for Achilles. It also appears that our sympathies with the valiant Siegfried in the first half are supposed to shift in the second half to the heroic deeds of his murderers, Hagen and Gunther. The epic is not even a history of a single dynasty or race. The Nibelungs are first one people, then another, then a third, depending on who controls the Nibelung treasure, which has become separated from the ring. As Richard Wagner concluded in his studies of the epic: 'the Hoard of the Nibelungen, as the epitome of earthly power, and he who owns it, who governs by it, either is or becomes a Nibelung.'

There are aspects of the medieval Nibelungenlied that are different from the more worldly ones portrayed in the Volsunga Saga. One is that the ring-hoard of the Volsunga Saga has suffered severe inflation by the time it reaches the Nibelungenlied. Gold among the Norsemen was a rare commodity. We find the golden hoard that Sigurd's horse Grani carried in the Volsunga Saga is so inflated in the Nibelungenlied that a baggage train consisting of hundreds of wagons is required to transport it.

There are also other curiosities about the epic. In the Volsunga Saga, the historical Attila the Hun is Atli, a savage and treacherous tyrant. However, in the Nibelungenlied, the Hun King known as Etzel is portrayed as a humane and sympathetic character. This is certainly because of the politics of the Austrian court for whom the Nibelungenlied was composed.

Christian morality and chivalric traditions also resulted in changes. The extreme courtly behaviour of the knights and the coyness concerning the defloration of Brunhild is at odds with the straight-forward Norse version. Also, there is undoubtedly a war-of-the-sexes aspect to the epic. Siegfried makes this clear in his battle with the Amazon. 'If I now lose my life to this girl, the whole sex will become uppish and never obey their husbands forever after,' he says. It does not seem to matter that Siegfried and Gunther cheat and lie to this obviously superior woman in the arena and in the bedroom. It all serves the higher moral purpose of keeping women subservient.

The warrior-maiden is also humbled and transformed – but more gently and without humiliation – in *The Lord of the Rings*. The shield maiden Éowyn who slew the Witch-king of Morgul is transformed by marriage into the gentle and subservient wife of Faramir; just as the unconquerable Amazon Queen Brunhild is transformed by marriage into the gentle and subservient wife of Gunnar.

The double standard is also vividly demonstrated in the last remarkable scene of the Nibelungenlied. Here the narrator suggests that the proper and chivalric attitude of Queen Kriemhild towards Hagen – the knight who murdered her husband, stole her treasure, and decapitated her only child – should have been mercy. When she demurs by cutting Hagen's head off with Siegfried's sword, her behaviour is seen as monstrous. In the chivalric tradition of the time, vengeance is a male prerogative and the slaying of even the vilest of knights by a woman is unforgivable. Immediately, a knight acts out the collective will of the court. He draws his own sword and executes her.

In the Nibelungenlied, the ring is obviously separated from the treasure before the tale properly begins. It is not with the treasure, but on the hand of the Amazon Queen. However, one aspect of the ring is taken on in the treasure trove by Tarnkappe, the cloak of invisibility that Siegfried wins by wrestling with the Dwarf Alberich. (In the same way the god Loki won the ring by wrestling with the Dwarf Andvari; and Frodo twice wrestled with Gollum for possession of the One Ring.) The trick of invisibility that the One Ring possesses is not present in Norse tales. In the Nibelungenlied Siegfried uses the Tarnkappe for invisibility against the Amazon; while both Bilbo and Frodo use the One Ring's invisibility against various enemies, dragons and wraiths.

It is important also to point out that even though the treasure and the cape of invisibility take over aspects of the ring's power, the ring remains the key to the epic's tragic plot. It is the ring taken by Siegfried from Brunhild and given to Kriemhild that ultimately seals the fate of all in the Nibelungenlied; just as surely as the movement of the One Ring seals the fate of all in *The Lord of the Rings.*

CHAPTER TEN

THE NIBELUNGENLIED

The national epic of the German race is the medieval Nibelungenlied, which is the 'Lay of the Downfall of the Nibelung Dynasty'. The Nibelungenlied is the Iliad of the Germanic peoples and was written by an anonymous poet around AD 1200 for performance in the Austrian court. The epic combines elements of myth with authentic historical events from the fifth century AD – the catastrophic annihilation of the once-powerful Burgundian peoples in the Rhineland by the Hun legions of Attila.

Although many medieval hero cycles use elements of the Norse Volsunga Saga, the Nibelungenlied is the most direct rendering of that particular tale. Siegfried is definitely the Norse Sigurd, Gunther is Gunnar, Kriemhild is Gudrun, Brunhild is Brynhild, and Hagen is Hogni. Besides the German, rather than Norse, names, the Nibelungenlied represents much more of a courtly medieval world than the more primitive Norse world of the Volsungs.

In *The Lord of the Rings*, as opposed to *The Hobbit* and *The Silmarillion* and its sequels, the world Tolkien defines has a closer affinity with the world of the medieval German knight Siegfried of the Nibelungenlied than that of the heroic warrior Sigurd of the Volsunga Saga. In the Volsunga Saga gods and dragons mix comfortably with mortal heroes; while in the courtly world of the Nibelungenlied epic, gods and dragons have no real place. Siegfried's early exploit of dragon-slaying takes place 'off stage', as it were. It is an event only talked about; more of an ancestral rumour than a real event. The dragon appearing on the medieval battlefield in the Nibelungenlied would be as incongruous as the god Odin turning up as a guest at Siegfried's marriage ceremony in Worms cathedral.

This is equally true of Aragorn's courtly kingdom of Gondor in *The Lord of the Rings*. Such events as the slaying of dragons also take place 'off stage': either in the fairy-tale world of *The Hobbit*, or the genuinely mythic world of *The Silmarillion*. As with the Nibelungenlied, it could equally be said that Smaug the Dragon appearing on a battlefield in *The Lord of the Rings* would be as incongruous as the Valarian god Manwë turning up as a guest at Aragorn's marriage ceremony in Gondor.

No investigation of the theme of the ring quest would be complete without reference to the Nibelungenlied. As with the Volsunga Saga, the story of this epic will be told in full without interjection or immediate comparison with Tolkien's *The Lord of the Rings*.

The Nibelungenlied is the tale of the rivalry of two queens. One is the gentle Queen Kriemhild who with three brothers rules the Burgundian kingdom of the Rhine. The other is Warrior-Queen Brunhild who alone rules in far Iceland. Both are maiden-queens of great beauty.

Queen Kriemhild's sleep is broken by a prophetic dream. In the dream a falcon is upon Kriemhild's jewelled wrist. This falcon is without equal; it is the most cherished of all things that Kriemhild calls her own. Yet, without warning, two eagles strike the bird in flight. Before Kriemhild's eyes, the eagles tear her falcon to pieces and glut themselves on its flesh.

Young Kriemhild comes to her mother who is a woman wise in the reading of dreams, but to her child she could give no comfort. The falcon is a prince whom Kriemhild will love and marry, while the eagles are two murderers who would destroy that prince.

And so, because of this dream, Kriemhild swears she will wed no man. Though many chivalrous knights desire her and sing her praises, she will wed no one. Nor are there any who might force her to wed, for her will is protected by her three brothers, the powerful Kings of Rhineland: Gunther, Gernot and Giselher.

Yet fate will not allow Kriemhild to keep her vow. North of the kingdom of the Rhine are the Netherlands and the great city of Xanten. There lives the hero Siegfried, the son of King Siegmund and Queen Sieglind. This is the mighty warrior who gained fame by travelling far to the north into the land of the Nibelungs, the richest kingdom in the world. There Siegfried slays the twelve guardian giants of Nibelungenland and takes from their armoury that ancient sword called Balmung, and with it defeats seven hundred men of Nibelungenland. At last he fights the two mighty Kings of the Nibelungs themselves, and in the din of combat, slays them both.

Yet the great treasure of the Nibelungs has one last guardian, more subtle and dangerous than all the rest. This is the ancient Dwarf Alberich who not only possesses huge strength but also wears the Tarnkappe, the Cloak of Invisibility. So Siegfried fights an invisible foe, but finally locks the Dwarf in his grip, overthrows him, and wins from him both the magic cloak and the Nibelung treasure.

So vast was the Nibelung treasure that it would take one hundred baggage wagons to carry away the precious stones alone; though these were but a scattering over the mounds of red gold that was heaped on the floors of the secret cavern where it was kept.

By force of arms, Siegfried becomes master of the Nibelung treasure and lord of Nibelungenland. And though Siegfried returns to Xanten to rule the Netherlands, he is acknowledged as the king of Nibelungenland as well. However, this is not the end of Siegfried's deeds, for besides countless combats against other men, this hero also slays a dragon. Further, by this deed Siegfried wins not just fame but invincibility. For after slaying the monster, he bathes in the dragon's blood, and his skin grows tough as horn so that no weapon can pierce him.

When Siegfried rides south in search of adventure, he comes to the land of the Burgundians, and there the three Kings of the Rhine greet him with honour. For the best part of a year Siegfried remains in Rhineland in the great city of Worms, and with King Gunther swears an oath of friendship. Still, there is another reason for Siegfried's journey. He has heard of the beauty of Kriemhild, and hopes he might win her as his queen.

Siegfried has reasoned well, for from her tower Kriemhild has often watched the hero in pageant and combat. By the sight of him alone, she is filled at once with love, and her resolve not to give her heart to any man is soon discarded.

As the year of Siegfried's visit approaches its end, there is a call to arms. The combined armies of the King of the Saxons and the King of the Danes are joined in huge force to make war on the Burgundians. Siegfried champions the Burgundian cause. So great is Siegfried's valour that although he leads a force of only one thousand knights, he crushes an army of twenty thousand Saxons and Danes in a single day.

Shortly after this great service to the Burgundians, Siegfried asks Gunther for his sister's hand in marriage. With gladness Gunther agrees, for he knows that his sister's heart is filled with love for this man, and that his kingdom has no stouter ally and friend. However, Gunther explains, one obstacle still stands before this union might be blessed. As Gunther is the eldest royal son and High

King of the Rhine, by the laws of the land he must be wed before his sister.

Now Gunther reveals that he is as enamoured of that other beautiful maiden-queen who rules in Iceland as Siegfried is of the fair Kriemhild. The only problem is that Queen Brunhild is no ordinary woman. She is a warrior-queen blessed with supernatural strength, and she swears that she will wed no man unless he can defeat her in three feats of strength. If a suitor tries and fails, he will be put to death. And though many suitors have tried to win Brunhild, all have failed and died.

So the bargain is struck. King Gunther will grant Queen Kriemhild's hand to Siegfried, if Siegfried helps Gunther win the beautiful Queen Brunhild. Siegfried and Gunther set sail for far Iceland. They take with them only two of Gunther's brave vassals: Hagen of Troneck and his brother Dancwart. This is a suitor's quest, and so they take no weapons of war, but array themselves in their finest clothes.

Queen Brunhild's fortress-city has eighty-six towers and three palaces, and her royal hall is built of sea-green marble. The travellers are graciously received by the Queen upon a throne all wreathed in silk and gold. She is as beautiful as all the tales have claimed. On her hand she wears an ancient red-gold ring and about her waist is a girdle adorned with precious gems: a splendid orphrey of fine silk braid from Nineveh.

Gunther's heart goes out to Brunhild at once, but it is to Siegfried that Brunhild speaks first. For the Queen assumes that Siegfried is the most noble of her visitors, and that it is he who has come as suitor. Here is the first of Siegfried's deceptions. To Brunhild, Siegfried falsely claims that he is a vassal to King Gunther, who is the greatest and strongest of heroes, and it is Gunther who comes to compete for her hand. With some reluctance the Queen accepts Gunther's challenge and agrees to the contest.

Queen Brunhild stands alone in the vast arena, surrounded by an iron ring of seven hundred men-at-arms who will judge the contest. The warrior-queen dresses herself in steel armour adorned with gold and gems. It takes four strong men to lift the Queen's bright shield, and three men to carry her spear: both of these she takes and wields like childish toys. Then into that arena marches her suitor and challenger, King Gunther of the Rhine. However, though he appears to stand alone against the warrior-queen, this is not so. The wily Siegfried has covered himself in Tarnkappe, his magic cloak, which not only makes him invisible, but has a second power, that of increasing the strength of its wearer twelvefold.

So, when the contest of the javelin is made, it is the invisible Siegfried who stands between Gunther and his shield and stops the force of the Queen's throw. Certain death would have been delivered to Gunther alone, for even with Siegfried's twelvefold strength, both heroes are staggered when the spear strikes and a tongue of flame leaps from the pierced shield. Brunhild is amazed when Gunther does not fall. Instead, Gunther appears to lift up her spear and, turning the blunt end to the fore – so as not to slay the maid – throws the weapon with such force as to drive her to the ground. But here Brunhild is deceived by appearance, for it was the invisible hand of Siegfried which hurled the spear.

Then come the next two tests: the casting of a great stone and the long leap. The stone is so heavy it takes twelve men to carry it into the arena. Without hesitation, Queen Brunhild lifts the stone and throws it the length of those twelve men laid end to end; then she makes a mighty leap that overshoots the distance of the stone.

In silent reply, Gunther goes to the stone and appears to lift it effortlessly, but once again it is the invisible Siegfried who does the deed and hurls the stone far beyond Brunhild's mark. Then, lifting Gunther by his waist, Siegfried leaps, carrying Gunther with him through the air, landing far beyond their stone-cast.

So, by the strength and cunning of Siegfried, Gunther has won a bride, and to the kingdom of the Rhine comes the proud Queen Brunhild. In Gunther's court at Worms there is much celebration and joy. There are to be two royal marriages: Gunther to Brunhild and Siegfried to Kriemhild.

Wedding guests are given gifts of bracelets, lockets and rings, while an iron ring of armed knights solemnly stands about the betrothed couples as they swear their holy vows. Joyfully, Gunther and Siegfried march out of the chapel with the two loveliest of brides. As night comes, they retire to their wedding beds, as their guests revel on.

In the morning, Siegfried and Kriemhild are radiant with their mutual love; while Gunther seems distraught, and Brunhild distant and aloof. Gunther has none of the bridegroom's natural joy and pride. Indeed, that very afternoon, Gunther comes to confide in Siegfried and tell him of his humiliation.

On their wedding night Brunhild tells Gunther that although he has won her hand by his skill in the arena, she will not willingly give up her body to him. For to give herself to a man would break the spell of her warrior's strength which she wishes to keep all her life. When Gunther tries by force to claim his nuptial rights, Brunhild merely laughs at him. She binds him up with her braided girdle, and hangs him like a slaughtered pig from a peg on the wall until dawn.

Once again Siegfried is drawn into an intrigue against the warrior-queen. That night in darkness, using Tarnkappe, his magic cloak of invisibility, Siegfried enters Brunhild's room. In Gunther's place he lies in Brunhild's bridal bed. Thinking it is Gunther in the dark, Brunhild strikes Siegfried with such force that blood leaps from his mouth and he is thrown across the room. Wrestling with the hero, Brunhild grips Siegfried's hands so tightly that blood spurts from his nails and he is driven against the wall. Yet finally, Siegfried's huge strength prevails. He lifts her from the ground, throws her down upon the bed, and by main force crushes her in his gathered arms so fiercely that all the joints of her body crack at once. Only then does she submit and cry out to her conqueror to let her live.

Now most who tell this tale say that at this moment Siegfried is an honourable friend to Gunther and does not rest in the lovely cradle of Brunhild's long limbs that night. But whatever the truth of the matter, in one way at least Siegfried does dishonour this proud woman. For in the darkness, Siegfried sees the dull glint of red gold. It is Brunhild's ring, and in his pride of conquest, he takes the ring from her hand. Then, as he leaves the marriage bed, he also takes the jewelled girdle of woven Nineveh silk as well.

In stealth, Siegfried flees the dark chamber, and Gunther comes to the bed of the vanquished bride who no longer dares to resist his advance. When the dawn comes, Brunhild is as pale and meek as the mildest bride. For with the loss of maidenhead and her ring, Brunhild's warrior strength flees her lovely body forever. She becomes a good and submissive wife to King Gunther.

Now twelve years pass happily. Siegfried and Kriemhild live and rule over the Netherlands and the Nibelungenland from their palace in Xanten; while Gunther and Brunhild live and rule over the Rhinelands. Then Gunther invites Siegfried and his sister to come to a festival in his court.

Perhaps the ancient power of the ring is at work, or perhaps the fault is in Siegfried's pride. Whatever the reason, Siegfried makes a tragic error, for in Xanten he gives as a gift the ring and the silken girdle he took from Brunhild in her wedding bed. And even more foolishly, he reveals to Kriemhild the secret of the winning of the ring and the girdle.

So one day, the two queens meet at the cathedral door and a dispute arises among them as to who should enter first. Brunhild is rash and maintains that Kriemhild has displayed unwarranted arrogance towards her; for obviously Siegfried is nothing more than a vassal of Gunther.

Kriemhild will not stand for this insult. She argues that Siegfried is the greater man and no man's vassal. Filled with exasperation, Kriemhild's discretion is abandoned. To Brunhild, she holds up the stolen ring of red gold, and then reveals the jewelled girdle of braided Nineveh silk that Brunhild once wore. Contemptuously, before all who will listen, she claims that Brunhild had been Siegfried's concubine before she wed Gunther; and that Siegfried had taken these trophies after he had been the first to enjoy her body upon the bridal bed.

The humiliated Brunhild flees to Gunther with this tale and demands that her honour be redeemed. Full of anger, Gunther calls Siegfried to him. Alarmed at this scandalous talk, Siegfried tells Gunther that what his wife has said is untrue and that he had not so used Brunhild that night. With no gentleness, Siegfried chastises his wife, and demands that she apologize for this shameful argument. In his haste to make amends so that Brunhild should not discover the other stratagems by which he deceived and subdued her, Siegfried orders an iron ring of knights to form about him, and swears a sacred oath that all these tales are black lies.

This false oath is the final seal on Siegfried's fate. His honour is despoiled. For although it seems that most accept this denial, the proof of the gold ring and the girdle cannot be withdrawn and rumour of the scandal of the marriage bed spreads. To Brunhild comes the steadfast Hagen of Troneck, the Queen's champion and the King's stoutest vassal. Brunhild inflames Hagen's heart, and these two persuade Gunther that only blood vengeance can restore their honour.

At this time rumours of war with the Danes again arise in the Rhine. Siegfried once again makes ready for war, but Kriemhild has dire forebodings. Artfully, Hagen comes to Kriemhild, saying that he too has had evil omens concerning her husband but that he cannot believe these omens as all know that Siegfried is protected by the spell of dragon's blood. It is then that Kriemhild reveals the secret of Siegfried's mortality. For when Siegfried bathed in dragon's blood, a lime leaf covered one place between his shoulder blades. In this place alone, Siegfried can be pierced with sharp steel. On Hagen's instructions, Kriemhild secretly sews a tiny cross on Siegfried's doublet over his one mortal place. Then Hagen swears he will always be at Siegfried's back, and will guard the hero from any unexpected blow.

The very next day, Hagen, Gunther and Siegfried go hunting in the royal forest. When Siegfried lies down to drink from a stream after a long chase, Hagen drives his spear into the cross and through Siegfried's back to his heart. Mortally wounded, Siegfried is like a wild, dying beast flailing the air. But after Hagen strikes, Gunther seizes Siegfried's weapons and flees, so the hero might not wreak vengeance with his final breath.

When at last Siegfried's life's blood spills out upon the forest floor and he breathes no more, the assassins return. They take up his body and carry it to the court proclaiming that Siegfried has been treacherously murdered by lawless highwaymen.

With Siegfried's death, Brunhild believes her honour has been upheld by her husband Gunther and her champion Hagen. Not only has she brought death to the man who deceived her, but the proud rival queen who had humiliated her is now brought to despair. Further, because Kriemhild is without a husband, Gunther takes her under his protection, and by this pretext plunders her inheritance, the Nibelung treasure.

In this treacherous way, the Burgundians make the Nibelung treasure their own. For days and nights an endless caravan of wagons filled with gold and jewels carries the vast treasure into the great walled city of Worms where Gunther and Brunhild rule. This treasure entirely fills the city's greatest tower. Yet so rich is this hoard that King Gunther mistrusts its keepers and others who might steal it. Stealthily over the years, under the cover of night, Gunther and Hagen pillage all that huge treasure and take it to a secret place on the Rhine. There Gunther and Hagen find a deep river cavern and sink all that vast treasure of gold and gemstones, so only these two in all the world know where it is hidden.

For a time the power and strength of Gunther's people are without parallel. With the Nibelung hoard in their possession, they are renowned as the wealthiest of nations. Indeed, because that famous treasure now rests in their land, the

Burgundians of the Rhine soon become known by all people as the Nibelungs: possessors of the Nibelungen treasure; the luckiest of men.

Not all within the kingdom are content. The grieving Kriemhild for one is not deceived by the tale of Siegfried's death. She guesses well enough the truth of his murder. Gradually her despair is replaced by a desire for revenge. Daily she stares at the gold ring on her hand which reminds her of the dispute that was the reason for her hero's treacherous murder.

At last Brunhild decides she can no longer have Kriemhild within the royal court, for she rightly fears that Siegfried's widow might ferment revolt. As chance would have it, Etzel the Emperor of the Huns of the Danube has sent word to the Nibelung court. The noble and elderly ruler of the Huns wishes to make the fair Kriemhild his queen. He has often heard of her beauty, and further he would be honoured to marry and protect the widowed queen of Siegfried the Dragonslayer.

To this proposal Gunther gives his blessing. He gives the hand of his sister to the Emperor Etzel and sends her to the Hun city of Gram on the banks of the Danube. Now Gunther believes that he and Brunhild might live forever secure from retribution for the slaying of Siegfried.

This is not to be. For although Kriemhild is taken to the mighty Huns' royal city of Gram and the palace of Etzel on the banks of the Danube, her desire for vengeance is never forgotten. Although the generous Etzel gives to her every luxury and she feigns happiness in his presence, Kriemhild works always towards one end.

The Emperor Etzel is quite unaware of Kriemhild's intrigues, and seems little concerned as his Queen comes to command greater and greater power among the Huns. She gains the sworn allegiance and obedience of great numbers of Etzel's vassals. Many knights out of compassion or love or greed swear loyalty to Kriemhild above all others.

After many years, when Kriemhild believes that her power is great enough, she persuades Etzel to invite all her kinsmen on a midsummer visit to the city of the Huns. So open-handed and fair has Etzel always been with the Nibelungs that they suspect no evil intent. So to Gram come the three Nibelung kings: Gunther, Gernot and Giselher; there also come the dauntless Hagen and his brother Dancwart; the mighty warriors Volker and Ortwine; and a thousand more heroic men as well. No nobleman is left within the walls of Worms, and from her tower Brunhild and her servants watch them go.

In the Emperor's city the midsummer celebrations are filled with pageantry and pomp. There are tournaments, games and festivals of song and dance. Yet the Nibelungs do not take part in the celebrations, for Gunther and Hagen see the fierce light of hatred that is in Kriemhild's eyes. Well they know its source, although they had hoped she had long ago laid her hatred to rest. Then, too, they have received ill omens on their long journey to the land of the Huns.

On the twelfth day of the journey, they came to the wide banks of the Danube. There Hagen came upon the swan maidens, those fatal river women who some call Nixies, and others call Watersprites. From them Hagen won a prophetic vision: all the Nibelungs by fire and sword would perish, and none would live to return to Rhineland.

So although all the Nibelungs had hoped that the Nixies had delivered to Hagen a false vision, the dreadful look of Kriemhild forewarns them of their doom. Thereafter they go about fully armed among the revellers. They do not have long to wait. That very night Kriemhild acts while all the Nibelung knights sit in the feasting-hall. Secretly, without Etzel's knowledge, Kriemhild sends a force of armed men to the quarters of the Nibelung squires, and all those valiant youths are slaughtered. When news of the slayings reaches the feast hall, Hagen leaps to his feet at the feasting-table. With relentless savagery, he draws his sword and strikes off the infant head of Ortlieb, Etzel's only child, as he plays upon his father's lap.

Then Hagen calls out to the Nibelungs, telling them they have fallen into a trap, that like the squires they too would all be slain. The Nibelung knights leap into battle and the hall becomes a slaughterhouse. Though Etzel and Kriemhild escape, two thousand Huns fall in that battle in the hall.

Much to Etzel's distress, Kriemhild urges on more of the Hunnish legions and allies. The feast hall is transformed: the tables are covered with severed limbs and heads, silver dishes are filled with human entrails, and gold cups brim with human blood. Kriemhild too is transformed; once the gentlest of women, she is now an avenging angel of death. Relentlessly, she urges the Huns into battle, and although more than half the Nibelungs have been slain, they hold the doors to the hall until a wall of bodies blocks the entrance, and the Huns have to clear their own dead to renew the fight.

Filled with fury, Kriemhild calls for torches and has the hall set ablaze to drive the Nibelungs into the open. But the fire does not drive the Nibelungs out, though many perish by flame and heat and smoke. They fight on through the blazing night. Taking refuge beneath the stone arches of the hall while the wooden structures burn about them, they battle on and drink the blood of the dead to slake their thirst.

Through the horror of that night a number of the Nibelungs survive, but with the dawn, the Queen calls forth many more grim Hunnish men-at-arms. These vengefully attack the Nibelungs in the burnt wreckage of the feasting-hall. Yet these warriors find even the remnants of the Nibelung knights a terrible foe, and many fall before their pitiless weapons.

Some of the Nibelungs might yet have lived had not that mighty hero, Dietrich the King of Verona, come to the aid of the Huns. Dietrich has no great desire to stand against the valiant Nibelungs; however, too many friends and kinsmen have now died at their hands. He knows he must act, so he sends his noble lieutenant Hildebrand with his men before him into the ruined hall. He asks Hildebrand to make some treaty between the Nibelungs and the Huns, so he himself need not be drawn into this feud.

But this act of reconciliation fails; the truce erupts at once in a bloody dispute that entirely eclipses both Dietrich's army and the ragged remainder of the Nibelungs. Only the wounded Hildebrand lives to return with the disastrous news. Grimly Dietrich arms himself and comes to the ruined hall to find that only the exhausted but defiant Gunther and Hagen remain alive of all the Nibelungs. In a rage of despair, Dietrich uses his mighty strength to drive the exhausted Gunther and Hagen to the wall. It might have been the ghost of Siegfried himself that had come, so great is his might. The weapons of the Nibelungs – even the sword Balmung which Hagen usurped – are struck from their hands, and they are subdued and bound by the fierce Dietrich.

Still Dietrich is a man of compassion, for he implores Kriemhild to have pity on these brave knights. For a moment, it seems that Kriemhild will hold back her wrath. In truth, Kriemhild has now become an avenging fiend gone far beyond redemption. In the throne-room she declares that there is yet the matter of her rightful inheritance to be resolved: the Nibelung treasure must be brought to Etzel's court.

In secret, Kriemhild has already been to the cells. She meets Hagen and makes to him a false promise of freedom if he will tell her where the Nibelung treasure is hidden. Hagen is a dark and stoic man, and he trusts not a word that Kriemhild speaks. Hagen tells the queen he has sworn an oath never to reveal where the Nibelung treasure is buried while his lord, Gunther, lives.

Queen Kriemhild orders Hagen to be brought in chains to the throne-room. Then, to the horror of all, Kriemhild throws the severed head of King Gunther – her own brother – upon the floor. The Emperor Etzel and the hero Dietrich are aghast at the Queen's savagery, but the fierce Hagen of Troneck defiantly laughs aloud.

There had been no oath of silence. Hagen had provoked the slaying because he feared that Gunther would trade his life for the treasure. But now that Gunther is gone, Hagen alone in all the world knows where that hoard is hidden, and no torture will ever make him tell. For if he cannot return the treasure to his Queen Brunhild, he can now at least deny that reward to her rival. Hagen laughs aloud, boasting that he would gladly suffer death and damnation to keep this last rich victory locked within his heart.

Hagen's defiance so enrages Queen Kriemhild that in an instant she takes into her hands Hagen's sword: the sword Balmung, which had once belonged to Siegfried. Then, before the Emperor or his courtiers can recover from the first shock of the unnatural murder of Gunther, Kriemhild strikes off the head of Hagen of Troneck as well.

All now see the monstrous being that Kriemhild has become. At this last act of treachery, all the royal court recoil in horror. All know that no greater shame can befall a knight than to be slain by the hand of a woman. It is Dietrich's lieutenant, Hildebrand, who acts out the will of all the assembled nobles when he leaps forward with his drawn sword. In a deed that might almost have been merciful, he ends the tortured life of Queen Kriemhild with a single stroke.

With the death of Hagen, the last Nibelung lord is slain and the Nibelung treasure is gone forever from the sight of men. The Nixies and Water Spirits of the Rhine alone know where it lies, and they have no use for gold or gems. The ancient ring that was the cause of all this despair is buried with Queen Kriemhild, who was once the gentlest of women; while her rival Queen Brunhild, who was once the strongest of her sex, is now broken by the loss of husband, champion and all wealth. She mourns the disaster that has extinguished all her noble men-at-arms and left her alone in a ruined and empty realm.

So ends the tale of the rivalry of the two queens.

CHAPTER ELEVEN

GREEK AND ROMAN MYTHS

There is one ancient Greek myth that tells of the forging of the first ring. The tale begins at the dawn of time, long before humans or even gods existed. In fact, the story of the first ring is bound up with the tale of the coming of the gods and the creation of man.

The Titans were the first race to rule the primeval world. They were the giant sons and daughters of Gaea, who is Mother Earth. Titans were as tall as the hills and both wise and strong. They also possessed magic powers with which they brought forth unlimited wealth and bounty.

The Titans gave birth to many children: sons and daughters who became the spirits of rivers and forests. All nature was animated by their offspring: the nymphs of the sea, the mermaids, the naiads, the satyrs and the sylphs.

One of the wisest of the Titans was gifted with the art of prophecy, and for this reason was named Prometheus, which means 'foresighted'. By this gift Prometheus had foreknowledge of the end of this age. He saw that by craft and cunning the Titans would be overthrown by the lesser race of the gods. Furthermore, he knew that his own fate was to be different from that of his soon-to-be-vanquished race; that it was to be bound up with that of these youthful gods.

When the war between the Titans and the gods was fought, it all but consumed the world. For ten long years the terror of that war racked the earth. From the height of Olympus, Zeus the storm god hurled down his thunderbolts; while his brother

Poseidon the sea god with his trident commanded the earth to quake. Rock ran in molten rivers. The sea boiled. Steam and flame filled the air. Great canyons gaped and continents split and shifted. Yet with their strength and magicians' powers, the Titans stood and fought the gods with glittering armour and shining spears. But valiant though they were, the Titans were overwhelmed by the gods. They were blasted by thunderbolts and the earth was rent from under them, causing them to fall into the deep pits of Tartarus where cruel Hades the god of the Underworld ruled and none could escape.

The Titan Prometheus was not condemned to such a fate as his brother, Atlas, who eternally held the weight of the heavens on his shoulders; nor indeed was he placed on the wheel of fire like Ixion; nor crushed by the weight of stone like Sisyphus; nor drowned in the abysmal boiling sea like many other Titans. Prometheus had taken no part in the war against the gods, and though he grieved for his people, he long had known their fate.

Prometheus went among the new gods and gave these harsh new rulers gifts of wisdom and knowledge. Prometheus turned his hand more and more to the arts of shaping metals and the substances of the earth he loved. He chose as a companion the lame son of Zeus called Hephaestos, the least haughty and overbearing of the gods. To Hephaestos he brought the fire and the forge, and with that god shared his deep knowledge of the earth. In the volcanic hearts of mountains Prometheus taught Hephaestos the skills of the forging of metals. There they forged jewelled crowns, sceptres and golden thrones for the gods of Olympus. They made bright weapons and armour blessed with magical powers. Hephaestos the Smith soon became so valued by Zeus that he gave the lame god the hand of Aphrodite, the beautiful goddess of love, in marriage.

Yet far-seeing Prometheus had also employed other crafts in his delving and forging. For the skills of the magician as well as the smith were endowed to those of the Titan race, so that in time the secret of life itself came to him. And, as is well known, Prometheus was the deity who shaped men from clay and breathed into them the breath of life. Furthermore, it was Prometheus who brought to men the gift of fire, for in their beginning they lived in darkness. With this gift of fire came also the light of wisdom and the heat of unquenchable desire, and all the things that make men greater than beasts and cause them to strive to achieve immortal fame.

The Olympian gods were greatly displeased, for they wished no rivals in the world, and claimed that Prometheus had given to the mortals what the gods alone should possess. Yet the act could not be undone and the fire could not be quenched. In wrath, Zeus commanded Hephaestos to forge a great chain of unbreakable adamantine, the iron of the gods. Then he commanded that Prometheus be taken into the Asian wilderness among the White Mountains between Scythia and Cimmeria, and upon the mountain called the Caucasus be chained. To that rock, Zeus swore, Prometheus would forever be bound. To Prometheus, Zeus sent a great eagle and a vulture of immense size. By these cruel birds, Prometheus's side was pierced and his liver torn out. Each night his liver grew again, only to be torn from him the next day. To him also came the fiery sun and the freezing rain and hail. Thus, like his brethren beneath the earth, Prometheus was filled with eternal pain.

Yet Prometheus endured and did not repent his deeds. By night came many nymphs, sylphs and spirits who grieved for him and sang soothing songs. Even some few of the race of men dared come to that terrible wilderness and seek his counsel. Yet none had the strength to break his bonds, and he seemed forever doomed to this torture.

As the long ages passed, it is said that the gods became less cruel, and though their treatment of men was not always fair or good, many among that mortal race they came to favour and even love. Between gods and men there grew a bond and a union, and from that union came many offspring. Mightiest of all of these was Heracles, the son of Zeus.

Zeus had come at last to regret his punishment of Prometheus. However, he was restrained by his own unbreakable oath of eternal bondage. However, when Heracles went into the Asian wilderness, Zeus did not drive him away from the White Mountains and allowed him to seek out Prometheus. Zeus knew that only Heracles possessed the strength to break the chains of adamantine; and the courage to slay the eagle and the vulture.

When Prometheus was at last freed, Zeus spoke to him in a voice of thunder. Zeus swore that he would both keep his oath of bondage, yet allow Prometheus to keep his freedom. So Zeus took from the chain of adamantine a broken link, and from Mount Caucasus he took a fragment of rock. With his immortal hand, Zeus welded the stone to the link. He then took the hand of Prometheus and about his finger he closed the link of adamantine. By this device Zeus kept his oath to chain the Titan to the rock of Caucasus forever, and yet he fulfilled his promise to let Prometheus walk free.

This was how the first ring was made. Afterwards, it is said, men came to wear rings to honour Prometheus, the bringer of fire and the father of man. It is claimed that the ring is a sign of the smith who is master of fire, and the magician who is master of life. And those who are kings of men wear the ring as a sign of their descent from Prometheus and the Titans who once ruled the earth.

In Prometheus, the good Titan who brought life and fire to the human race, we have a mirror opposite to Tolkien's Sauron, the evil sorcerer who brought death and darkness. However, when Sauron appeared in the Second Age in disguise among the Elven-smiths of Eregion as the mysterious stranger Annatar the Lord of Gifts, he must have seemed everything to the Elves that Prometheus was to humans. For Annatar the Lord of Gifts was also a magician-smith who like Prometheus defied the gods by giving away forbidden gifts of knowledge and skill. With Annatar's guidance Celebrimbor and the Elven-smiths of Ost-in-Edhil in Eregion learned secrets of the smith and the magician matched only by the Valarian gods themselves. Only after Annatar tricked the Elves into forging the Rings of Power did they learn the terrible price of Annatar's gifts. The price demanded of Prometheus's gifts was that the Titan himself be eternally bound and enslaved. The price demanded of Sauron's gifts was that the Elves be eternally bound and enslaved.

The Greek legend of the first ring obviously links the ring to many primal images of power which later emerge in the ring quest tradition and are obviously linked with alchemy and metallurgy. In this tale, the first ring is solidly connected with the powers of the magician and the smith. Curiously, Prometheus, the father of man, the giver of fire and the master of smiths, has a ring forged of iron in the Caucasian Mountains: the very place where the secret of iron-smelting was discovered.

Tolkien read Latin and Greek and had an extensive knowledge of Greco-Roman myth and history. However, Tolkien's mythology of Middle-earth was intentionally rooted in northern European mythic traditions, rather than Mediterranean ones. Nonetheless, just as there are aspects of the Greco-Roman tradition to be found in Teutonic and Celtic legends, so there are aspects of the Greco-Roman tradition evident in Tolkien's tales.

In looking at the rise and fall of the Roman Empire, we have already pointed out many historical similarities with Tolkien's history of the United Kingdom of the Dúnedain. The history of Gondor as the capital of the southern Dúnedain kingdom and Arnor as the capital of the northern Dúnedain kingdom is comparable to the history of Constantinople as the capital of the eastern Roman empire and Rome as the capital of the western Roman empire. Tolkien's fiction featured Easterling barbarian hordes (in the service of the evil eye of Sauron the Necromancer) who constantly menaced the Dúnedain empire's eastern borders. This is comparable to the Teutonic barbarian hordes (in the service of the one-eyed god Woden the Necromancer) who constantly menaced the Roman empire's eastern borders. Gondor's great rivals to the south were the lords of Umbar, whose mighty war fleets were the terror of the seas and whose powerful mercenary armies were supported by war-elephants and were a terror on land. This is comparable to ancient Rome's great rivals to the south who were the lords of Carthage, whose mighty war fleets were the terror of the seas and whose powerful mercenary armies were supported by war-elephants and were a terror on land.

One of the most obvious connections between the legends of the ancient Greeks and Tolkien's imaginative fiction lies in the story of Atlantis. Tolkien's account of the 'Akallâbeth' or 'The Downfall of Númenor' is his reinvention of the Atlantis legend. This was one very distinct case of Tolkien taking an ancient legend and rewriting it in such a way as to suggest that this is the real history on which the myth was based. So as not to miss the point, Tolkien tells us the High Elven (Quenya) form of Númenor is 'Atalantë'.

Tolkien often mentioned that he had 'an Atlantis complex' in the form of a 'terrible recurrent dream of the Great Wave, towering up, and coming in ineluctably over the trees and green fields.' He appears to believe this to have been some kind of racial memory of the ancient catastrophe of the sinking of Atlantis. He stated on more than one occasion that he believed he inherited this dream from his parents, and later found that it had been passed on to his son, Michael. In *The Lord of the Rings* he gives exactly this nightmare to Faramir, the son of the last Steward of Gondor.

In his writing of 'The Downfall of Númenor', however, Tolkien found he had managed to exorcize this disturbing dream. Evidently the dream had not recurred since he dramatized the event in his own tale of the catastrophe.

The original legend of Atlantis comes from Plato's 'Timaeus' in which an Egyptian priest talks to the Athenian statesman Solon. The priest tells Solon that the mightiest civilization the world had ever known existed nine thousand years before his time in the island-kingdom of Atlantis. Atlantis was an island about the size of Spain in the western sea beyond the Pillars of Heracles. Its power extended over all the nations of Europe and the Mediterranean, but the overwhelming pride of these powerful people brought them into conflict with the immortals. Finally, a great cataclysm in the form of a volcanic eruption and a tidal wave resulted in Atlantis sinking beneath the sea.

Tolkien used Plato's legend as an outline for 'The Downfall of Númenor'. However, Tolkien seemed incapable of doing what most authors would do by simply writing a straight dramatic narrative based on the legend. Typically, he just couldn't seem to help adding little personal touches and background details: like the compilation of three thousand years of detailed history, sociology, geography, natural history, linguistics, and biography for Númenor!

Curiously, the founder of Tolkien's lost realm of Númenor is linked to another quite separate Greek myth. The first Númenórean king, Elros, and his twin brother Elrond, were the twin sons of a mortal man and an immortal Elven maid. Because of their mixed blood, the Half-Elven twins were forced to choose their people and their fate: the mortal world of Men, or the immortal world of Elves. Elrond chose to be immortal and eventually became the Elf Lord of Imladris. His brother Elros chose to be mortal and became the founding king of the Númenóreans.

Elros and Elrond are comparable to the Greek myth of twin brothers Castor and Pollux. These heroes were the twin sons of the mortal woman Leda, and the immortal god Zeus. In this case, Castor was a mortal man and Pollux was an immortal god. When the mortal brother Castor was slain in battle, and the immortal brother Pollux was filled with grief because he could never be reunited with his brother, even in the Underworld, Zeus took pity on the them, and transformed the brothers into the constellation Gemini, the Heavenly Twins.

Tolkien's brothers are not reunited by being placed among the stars. However, there is a star connection in the figure of Elros and Elrond's famous father, Eärendil the Mariner. (Eärendil was originally an obscure figure from Teutonic myth, which Jacob Grimm associates with the morning star.) In Tolkien's tales Eärendil the Mariner binds the shining Silmaril to his brow and forever rides his flying ship through the firmament, where in the form of the morning star he guides all sailors and travellers.

In *The Lord of the Rings*, during the siege of Gondor there is one episode that most exactly mirrors the climax of the Greek myth of Theseus and the Minotaur. In the Greek tale, the Athenian hero Theseus sets out in a black-sailed tribute ship to Crete where the young prince along with other Athenian youths is to be taken and sacrificed to the monstrous Minotaur in the palace of King Minos. Upon departure, Theseus promises his father, the king of Athens, that if he slays the Minotaur and releases his people from bondage, he will change the sails to white as a signal of victory. In the flush of his triumph, however, Theseus forgets his promise. Tragically, his father sees the black-sailed ship returning. Believing his son to be dead, and his nation still enslaved, the king throws himself from a high cliff into the sea.

In *The Lord of the Rings*, we have Denethor, the Ruling Steward of Gondor, who sees the black-sailed ships of the enemy Corsair fleet sailing up the Anduin River at a critical moment in the Battle of Pelennor Fields. At this time Denethor's oldest son is slain, and he believes his surviving son is about to die.

He is correct in assuming that enemy reinforcements in the black-sailed ships would make the defence of Gondor impossible. Denethor goes mad with grief and despair and commits suicide, but like Theseus's father, Denethor is tragically mistaken. He does not know that the black-sailed ships of the Corsairs have been captured by Aragorn, who brings allies of Gondor to the field, which turns the battle in Gondor's favour. Just as Athens wins its freedom and Theseus succeeds his father, so Gondor wins its freedom and Denethor's son Faramir succeeds his father.

Although most aspects of Tolkien's world and cosmology are comparable to those of the northern European races, in his gods, the Valar, there are many parallels with the Greco-Roman pantheon of Olympian gods. Tolkien's king of the gods is Manwë the Lord of the Air, who rules from his throne and temple on the top of Taniquetil, the tallest mountain in the world. The eagle is sacred to Manwë, who is a fierce, bearded god of storms. He is very like Zeus – whom the Romans called Jupiter – the king of the gods who ruled from his throne and temple on the top of Olympus, the tallest mountain in the world. The eagle was also sacred to Zeus, who was the fierce, bearded god of storms.

Manwë's mightiest brothers, Ulmo, the god of the sea, and Mandos, the god of the dead, had direct counterparts in Greco-Roman mythology. Ulmo shares most of his characteristics with Poseidon, the Greek god of the sea – whom the Romans called Neptune. Both were giant bearded sea-lords who drove foaming sea chariots pulled by sea-horses on the crest of a tidal wave. Mandos shares many characteristics with Hades, the Greek god of the dead – whom the Romans called Pluto. Both ruled over a House of the Dead in a subterranean Underworld, and both knew the fates of mortals and immortals alike.

Among the Valarian goddesses Yavanna, who is the queen of the earth, and her young sister Vána, who is the queen of the blossoming flowers, have direct parallels in the Greco-Roman pantheon. The Greek earth-mother goddess is Demeter – whom the Romans called Ceres – while her daughter is the goddess of spring, Persephone – whom the Romans called Proserpine.

To Tolkien's Valarian god Aulë the Smith, we have an exact counterpart in the Greek Hephaestos the Smith – whom the Romans called Vulcan. Both were capable of forging untold wonders from the metals and elements of the earth. Both were armourers and jewellers to the gods. Other Valarians who are comparable to Greco-Roman gods are: Tulkas the Strong, who shares many characteristics with the Greek strongman Heracles (the Roman Hercules); and Oromë the Hunter, who bears a partial resemblance to the Greek celestial hero, Orion the Hunter.

The Greek god Hades and his Roman counterpart Pluto are not only comparable to the stern but relatively benign Mandos, but on the darker side, they share some characteristics with Tolkien's evil Valarian Melkor, who becomes Morgoth the Dark Enemy. This is Hades – or Pluto – in his most vilified form as the lord of the Underworld. This is the Hades who torments the dead; who kidnaps Persephone and risks bringing the eternal darkness of winter to the world. He is the lord of the Underworld who has to be tricked into releasing captured souls.

This is the Hades of the Greek love story Orpheus and Eurydice, which is mirrored in the adventures of Tolkien's lovers Beren and Lúthien in *The Silmarillion*. In that tale, Lúthien sang and made Carcharoth the wolf-guardian fall asleep before the gates of Morgoth's dark, subterranean kingdom. Once within, Lúthien again sang such beautiful songs that she and Beren won the Silmaril jewel from Morgoth the Lord of the Underworld. Lúthien succeeded in fleeing from the Underworld, but at the last moment, at the mouth of the tunnel, she lost her lover Beren. Although male and female roles are reversed, this is largely a retelling of the Greek myth. Orpheus played his harp and sang to make Cerberus the hound-guardian fall asleep before the gates of Hades' dark, subterranean kingdom. Once within, Orpheus again sang such beautiful songs that he won the life of Eurydice from Hades the Lord of the Underworld. Orpheus succeeded in fleeing the Underworld, but at the last moment, at the mouth of the tunnel, he lost his lover Eurydice.

To underline the connection between the Greek myth and his tale, Tolkien duplicates the journey by having Lúthien pursue Beren's soul after his death. This time, in the real House of the Dead in the Undying Lands, Lúthien exactly repeats Orpheus's journey by singing to Mandos-Hades and winning a second life for her lover. Unlike Orpheus and Eurydice, however, Lúthien and Beren are allowed to live out their newly won mortal lives.

The aspects of Hades that are comparable to the evil Morgoth the Dark Enemy are also manifest in an early Roman version of Pluto. This early Roman ruler of the dead was a demonic being called Orcus. Curiously enough this Latin 'Orcus' as the god of dead spirits or demons was the root for the Old English word 'Orc', meaning 'demon'. Coming full circle, it was this same Old English word 'Orc' which Tolkien used to name that evil race of demon goblins who were bred and enslaved by their infernal master, Morgoth the Dark Enemy.

CHAPTER TWELVE

BIBLICAL LEGENDS

The contribution of Judeo-Christian tradition to Tolkien's imaginative writing is both paradoxical and – in one particular legend – profound. In many respects, the early Judeo-Christian world is very unlike Tolkien's world. Tolkien purposely created a world that was without formal religion. Although Tolkien's characters did not quite worship the Valarian gods, their beliefs were very much closer to the pantheism of the pagan Teutons, Celts and Greeks than they were to the fierce monotheism of the Old Testament Hebrews.

However, in Tolkien's tales of creation of his world of Arda in *The Silmarillion* and subsequent books, we see can see biblical language and themes that add an undeniable grandeur to the event. In his creation tales we also see that behind the multiplicity of appearance, Tolkien conceived a primal cause in the form of a single entity, which is not far removed from the Judeo-Christian monotheistic God. In Tolkien's Eru the One – whom the Elves call Ilúvatar – all things entered the great Void of space. In the beginning these were his 'thoughts' in the form of the Ainur or 'Holy Ones'. These vastly powerful Ainur spirits were given life and independent powers, and in the Timeless Halls Ilúvatar commands them to sing in a celestial choir. This is known as the Music of the World, out of which all things come.

Most powerful of the mighty Ainur spirits was the magnificent Melkor, who – being the lord of darkness – saw things differently. This resulted in his disruption of the celestial music, and ultimately a war of powers in the heavens, which is later transferred to a war of powers on earth.

Once the Ainur spirits enter Arda, they are transformed and become the Valarian gods who strongly resemble the early pagan gods of Olympus and Asgard. However, in their early celestial manifestations, the Ainur are very like powerful Judeo-Christian Angels and Archangels. Certainly the grand conflict that arises between the Eru and Melkor owes much to the war between God and his rebel angel, Satan, as portrayed in John Milton's 'Paradise Lost'. Melkor's revolt both in its celestial form and within the spheres of the world greatly resembles the cataclysmic War in Heaven, when Satan led his rebel angels against the Angels of God.

In character and deeds, Melkor is very like John Milton's Satan, who is destroyed by pride and ultimately damned. His is very much a case of one who, like Milton's Satan would rather 'reign in Hell, than serve in Heaven.'

Melkor the Lord of Darkness, and his eventual successor, Sauron the Dark Lord, make war on Ilúvatar by proxy within the spheres of the world. Their grudge with Ilúvatar drives them on to destroy and corrupt all that He has created. This is the basis for all conflict on Tolkien's Middle-earth and results in a morality of absolute good and evil. Although Tolkien's world is a pagan one, the absolute sense of good versus evil and darkness versus light in his writing has its root inspiration in the Judeo-Christian tradition.

Beyond the philosophical comparisons, however, the strongest links between biblical legends and Tolkien's tales relate to beliefs in the power of rings. By biblical times, all kingdoms and nations had long accepted the tradition of the ring as a symbol of a monarch's authority. The king's ring not only marked him as the monarch, but the ring could be said to possess power in itself. Often, in the absence of the king, the ring or the ring's seal could be used to carry the full authority of the ruler. In such a way, the king might make a proclamation over all his lands, or delegate authority to his servants and subjects.

These rings of authority were made in many forms. Most often they were signet rings inscribed or marked with the symbol and name of their master on fixed seals of stone, crystal, amber or even hard gems. These could then make the mark of the king's seal with ink, or on wax or clay. Assyrian monarchs wore rings with engraved cylinder seals set in roller bezels. Some carried no marking at all, but in some such cases the properties of the sacred stone or precious metal carried their authority.

The pharaohs of Egypt wore the great scarab ring of ebony stone inlaid with gold. The scarab was set on a swivel bezel so it might be turned to reveal the cartouche: the great seal of the Pharaoh. Control of the ring brought control of Egypt, for the seal was the word of the Pharaoh, and the word of the Pharaoh was sacred law.

In the Old Testament is the tale of Joseph, who was given the Pharaoh's ring to rule over all Egypt. Joseph was sold by his brothers into slavery, and was betrayed by his master's wife and thrown into prison. Yet because Joseph proved so wise in the interpretation of dreams he was finally brought before the Pharaoh and called upon to interpret two prophetic dreams. Although no magician or holy man in Egypt was able to read the Pharaoh's visions, Joseph succeeded in this task. The Pharaoh saw that the wisdom of Joseph was so great that he made him his chief counsellor. In his great chambers, with a thousand servants bowed before him, the Pharaoh put out his hand to Joseph. 'And the Pharoah took off his ring from his hand, and put it upon Joseph's hand, and arrayed him in vestures of fine linen and put a gold chain about his neck. Then the Pharoah said to Joseph: 'Without thee no man shall lift up his hand or foot in all the land of Egypt.'

Besides Joseph, many other Hebrew heroes and leaders were associated with rings of supreme authority or power. In the middle ages, Moses, who led the exodus of the Hebrews out of Egypt back to the promised land of Israel, was commonly associated with the use of magic rings.

The use of magic rings apart, Tolkien draws a biblical parallel in *The Silmarillion* between his Elves and the Hebrew tribes of Moses. Like Moses' people, the Elves are a 'chosen people' who endure terrible hardships of mass migration to a 'promised land'. The 'Great Journey' of the Elves across the wildernesses of Middle-earth is to Eldamar, the promised homeland of the Elves in the Undying Lands; just as the Hebrews come to Israel, the promised home-land of the Jews. Both are comparable in that they are divinely summoned: the Elves by the god Manwë; the Hebrews by the god Jehovah. Much later, Tolkien describes a second migration of the Noldor Elves back to Middle-earth which is also reminiscent of the Hebrew exodus. However, it differs in that the Hebrew's leader, Moses, acted at the command of his god, Jehovah, while the Elves' charismatic leader, Fëanor, acted against the command of his god, Manwë.

If Tolkien uses certain biblical themes that connect his Elves with the Hebrews, it is also evident that his mortal Númenóreans resemble the biblical Egyptians. Tolkien states this directly and in detail in one of his letters of the late 1950s.

> The Númenóreans of Gondor were proud, peculiar, and archaic, and I think are best pictured in (say) Egyptian terms. In many ways they resembled 'Egyptians' – the love of, and power to construct, the gigantic and massive. And their great interest in ancestry and in tombs. (But not of course in 'theology': in which respect they were Hebraic and even more puritan.)... I think the crown of Gondor (the South Kingdom) was very tall, like that of Egypt, but with wings attached, not set straight back but at an angle. The North Kingdom had only a diadem – cf. the difference between the North and South Kingdoms of Egypt.

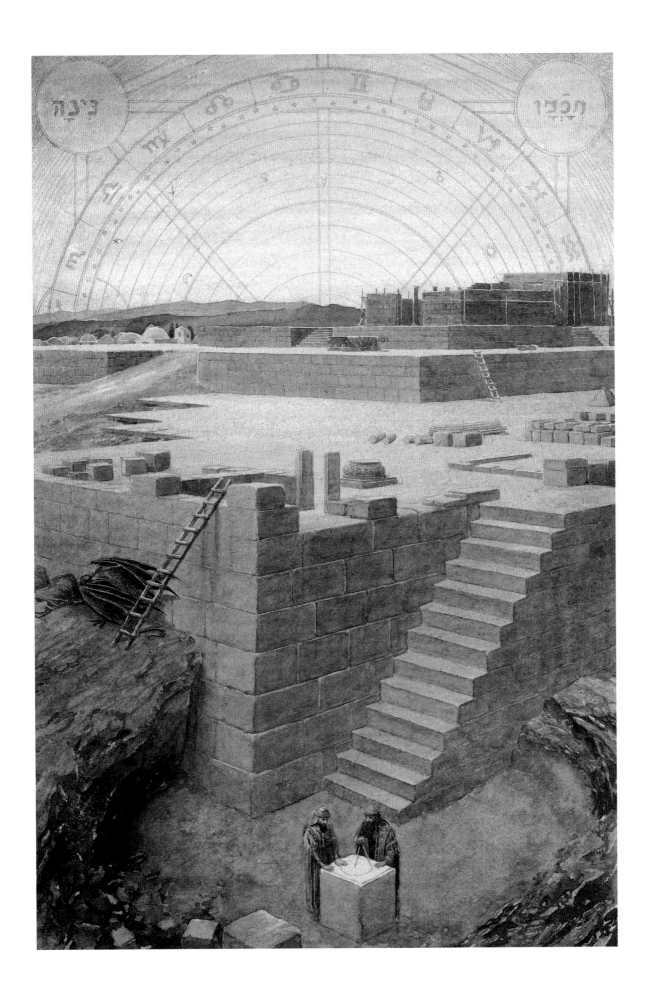

The destruction of Númenor itself rather echoes the biblical cataclysm when the Pharoah of Egypt's army pursues the Hebrews of Moses who are fleeing to the Chosen Land. Because he will not recognize the authority of the Hebrew god, the Pharaoh and his mighty army are swallowed up by the waters of the Red Sea. This is comparable to the King of Númenor whose navy follows the sea roads of the Elves to the Undying Lands. Because he won't recognize the authority of the Valarian god, the King of Númenor and his mighty navy are swallowed up by the waters of the western sea.

The most famous ring legend in the Judeo-Christian tradition was one that is linked with King Solomon. Tradition tells us that Solomon was not only considered a powerful king and wise man, but was also believed to be the most powerful magician of his age. These magician's powers were attributed largely to his possession of a magic ring. The legend of 'King Solomon's Ring' is certainly the one tale of the Judeo-Christian tradition that had the most profound influence on the imagination of Tolkien in his composition of *The Lord of the Rings*.

There can be little doubt that Tolkien was familiar with this ancient biblical tale of a sorcerer-king who (like Sauron) used a magic ring to command all the demons of the earth, and bent them to the purpose of ruling his empire. Just as Solomon uses his magic ring to build his great temple on Moriah, so Sauron uses the One Ring to build his great tower in Mordor. Of all rings of legend and myth, Solomon's Ring most resembles the One Ring of *The Lord of the Rings*.

Solomon's Ring is also like Sauron's One Ring in that its power can corrupt its master; even one as wise as Solomon. In the figure of the demon Asmodeus we see the subtle agent of evil who corrupts the wise but fatally proud King Solomon of Israel, and through possession of the ring causes his downfall. In the figure of the demon Sauron we see the subtle agent of evil who corrupts the wise but fatally proud King Ar-Pharazôn of Númenor, and through possession of the ring causes his downfall.

Curiously, the tale of Solomon's Ring also has elements that invite comparison with that other miraculous quest object of Tolkien's mythology. Just as the Elven King Thingol succeeds in acquiring the brilliant, light-radiating jewel called the Silmaril, so the Hebrew King Solomon succeeds in acquiring the brilliant, light-radiating jewel called the Schamir. Both are heirlooms of their races: the Silmaril was once the sacred jewel of the ancestral leader of the Elves, Fëanor; while the Schamir was the sacred jewel of the ancestral leader of the Jews, Moses. In Tolkien, the Silmaril is finally set into a gold headband, and shines from the brow of the celestial traveller, Eärendil the Mariner, in the form of the morning star. Once the Schamir is returned to the Hebrews, the radiant jewel appears to fit perfectly on the golden bezel of Solomon's Ring. The jewel doubles the power of Solomon's Ring, and illuminates the 'One Name' of God.

The story of how the ring came to Solomon is bound up with the tale of the building of the Temple of Yahweh, the Lord God Almighty. Solomon had set the slaves of Israel and the craftsmen of Tyre to work on the wondrous Temple of Mount Moriah, but Yahweh had forbidden the use of iron in its construction. Although a great multitude strove to build the Temple, its growth was slow. The slaves and craftsmen laboured longer and longer each month, but it was as if nothing was accomplished and each day the king's builders grew paler and thinner. At last one named Jair, who was a master builder and Solomon's favourite slave, came to him. Once young and vigorous, Jair was now shrunken and utterly emaciated. Each night, he claimed, a vampire came and sucked his blood and the blood of his workmen. And the same demon spirited away food and gold, and materials of marble, cedar and stone.

Deeply troubled, Solomon climbed to a high jutting rock on Mount Moriah and prayed unto Yahweh. Suddenly the emerald-winged archangel Michael, in a vision of brilliant light, appeared before him bearing a gold ring and said: 'Take, O Solomon, King, son of David, the gift which the Lord God, the highest Zebaot, hath sent unto thee. With it thou shalt lock up all the demons of the earth, male and female; and with their help thou shalt build up Jerusalem. But thou must wear this seal of God.'

Solomon was amazed but took into his hands the ring which was small and of pure gold. On the bezel of the ring was the seal of God: the five-pointed star of the pentalpha and the four letters of the name of Yahweh (YHWH). This was the ring from beneath the throne of God that some claimed had been Adam's before the fall of Man, and others claimed was Lucifer's before the expulsion of the rebel angels.

Standing alone on Mount Moriah, Solomon slid the ring onto his finger and suddenly he was filled with the sound of a great music. It was the music of the many spheres of the universe in the symphony of their turning. He was possessed now of an understanding of life and beauty beyond the grasp of other mortals. By the power of the ring he understood the language of the birds, animals and fish. He could talk with the trees and herbs and knew the deep secrets of earth and stone. Within the world nothing was hidden from him.

Armed with the ring, Solomon now dared to employ its greatest powers and summoned the vampire Ornias who had weakened Jair and frustrated the building of the Temple. He told Ornias that he must compensate him by cutting stones by day for the Temple, and Ornias bowed low and obeyed the command of the ring lord. But first Solomon asked Ornias, who was the lord of all the demons? Ornias answered 'Beelzebul'. Solomon gave Ornias the ring and told him to summon Beelzebul to his presence. Ornias took it, went to Beelzebul and said, 'Hither, Solomon calls thee.' And Beelzebul laughed and said, 'Who is this Solomon?' Then Ornias threw the ring at Beelzebul's breast, saying: 'Solomon the King summons you under the seal of Yahweh.' Beelzebul cried aloud with a mighty voice, emitted a great flame and came into Solomon's presence.

So did Beelzebul, proud lord of the demons, bow low before the feet of the master of the ring and await his pleasure. At Solomon's command Beelzebul summoned all the demons of the earth before the king. Never had so many great spirits been gathered at the command of a mortal. There were demons of two kinds: the common demons of the mortal earth who are the spirits of disease; and the sons of Heaven, fallen.

In the first group were the thirty-six 'Decani', the genii of sickness for every part of the body, and the seven who in the shape of stars cause moral sickness. All of these were deformed and ghastly. Upon them Solomon set his seal and they fell afflicted with their own maladies. Then he imprisoned them in copper cylinders. Some say that no man fell sick until the Temple was finished; others that there was no more sickness until the Chaldeans sacked the Temple, opened the bottles in ignorance, and inflicted sickness once more upon the world.

In the second group were the fallen angels in many forms. There was Rabdos, who travelled the earth in a dog's likeness and always had a dog's head. There was the Pterodrakon and the three-headed dragon. There was Envy, who had the limbs of man and no head, and in consequence ate people's minds in his search for a head. There were the three Liliths, beautiful enchantresses: Onoskelis the fair-skinned and naked; Enepsigos the winged; and Obyzuth the serpent-tailed; together with the hermaphroditic Akephalos who had eyes for nipples. There was Epiphas the great wind, Kunopeigos the lord of the Red Sea, Lix Terrax the Sandstorm; and many others of changed or combined shapes: asses' ears above the manes of lions; elephants' trunks under the wings of bats; vultures' talons in the scales of fish; toothed feet; headed arms; and some composed all of entrails and organs. And though Beelzebul was their lord, he was not Solomon's chief adversary among all the demons. This was the great Asmodeus: tall, mocking, sardonic and handsome, albeit bat-winged and cloven-footed.

Before this terrible host Solomon raised his hand adorned with the gold ring and he commanded them all to work upon the Temple of Yahweh. Those who rebelled were shut under the great seal into jars, like the demons of disease. So at this time Solomon used the power of the ring only to achieve the work of Yahweh and all went well with him and his kingdom. But still, because of God's prohibition of iron, the building went slowly, for the cutting of the great stones of the Temple was long and difficult work.

Solomon held counsel with his wise men, and the scholars among them told him of that brilliant and magical gem called the Schamir which Moses had used to engrave the names of the tribes of Israel upon the precious stones of the High Priest's ephod. They claimed that the power of this gem was so great it could cut any substance. But neither the scholars nor the demons could tell Solomon where the Schamir could be found. Only Asmodeus possessed this knowledge and during Solomon's absence he had escaped. Yet Solomon pursued and trapped him, and with the ring forced him to reveal where the Schamir might be found. Asmodeus said that the Schamir had been entrusted to the Angel of the Sea after Moses' death, and that it was now under the protection of the Sea Eagle. Solomon searched out the nest of this gigantic and deathless bird and laid a dome of crystal over it. When the Sea Eagle came and could not reach her young, she flew off and returned with the Schamir. She placed it on the crystal which instantly shattered. The slaves of Solomon appeared and cast spears and bolts of iron at the Sea Eagle. In fright she fled and the slaves retrieved the magical gem that could cut rock like butter.

The Schamir fitted exactly upon the bezel of Solomon's gold ring. Through it the pentalpha and the One Name could be seen, shimmering and pulsating with such colour and radiance that some have claimed that the ring was also set with diamond, sapphire, emerald and ruby. But in truth there was only one gem, and by its power the rock of the temple was cut.

Yahweh spoke in the night to Solomon, warning him that the power of his ring was now doubled. He told Solomon that he must no longer ignore Michael's first instruction to wear the ring at all times. It would preserve him from harm and keep him on the throne.

After the finding of the Schamir, Asmodeus was kept under bonds by Solomon in his palace. And from him the king learnt many secrets of the future for the fallen sons of Heaven, who are the stars of the zodiac, eavesdrop at the gates of Heaven, and hear the plans of Yahweh and his angels. But Solomon underestimated Asmodeus, who had never told him the full truth about God's workings, but instead lulled him into a false security. Moreover, with the Temple finished, Solomon paid more attention to pleasure than to piety; and Yahweh will not be mocked.

One day Asmodeus enraptured the king with a tale of the power and visions of the demons. Solomon asked how they could be so happy and gifted if a mere mortal like himself could keep their greatest prince under bonds. Asmodeus answered that Solomon had only to loosen his fetter and lend him the ring and he would prove his power and ecstatic vision. Solomon agreed. Asmodeus took the ring and placed it on his hand. By its doubled power the demon rose like a mountain before Solomon until one wing touched Heaven and the other touched the Earth. He snatched up Solomon and hurled him out of Israel into the vast wilderness of the south.

Some legends say that Asmodeus then passed himself off as the king, but the authoritative version reveals that he conjured up a counterfeit Solomon who appeared in every way like the king (though some of his wives and concubines were puzzled and troubled by their lord's strange new appetites). Asmodeus himself flew out of Israel and returned to the freedom of his mountain fastness, hurling the ring into the depths of the Red Sea.

For three years Solomon wandered, an unrecognized beggar, atoning for his sins, while a counterfeit king sat on the throne. He came to the city of Ammon, took service as a kitchen skivvy in the palace of its king, and proved so talented that he was made chief cook. The king's daughter, Naamah, fell in love with Solomon and the Ammonite king had the lovers taken to the desert to starve.

But Solomon still knew the language of the wild things and by his wisdom he and Naamah found enough food and water to survive until they came to the sea. There Solomon helped a fisherman draw in his nets to the shore and he was rewarded with a fish. When Naamah cleaned the fish she found a ring in its belly – the ring that Asmodeus had cast into the sea. Solomon put on the ring, gave thanks to Yahweh, and transported himself and Naamah to Jerusalem in a trice. The counterfeit Solomon fell before the true king and vanished under the ring's seal.

The true Solomon was restored to his kingdom and his great wealth. Yet as time passed, Solomon became once again corrupted. he grew lustful and hedonistic and thus fell from grace with Yahweh. He began sacrificing to the gods of his various wives as well as to the Hebrew God. Above all he was besotted with his Jebusite queen and used his ring to build her goddess, Ashtaroth, a great temple and idol on the slopes of Mount Moriah.

Then Asmodeus, who was his evil tempter in all this, brought word from his eavesdropping at Heaven's gate that the kingdom would be split at Solomon's death; that the Temple and his books would be destroyed, and that the demons of disease would be released again.

Solomon repented, but it was too late and Asmodeus's prophecies came about. However, it is said that Solomon died upright, leaning on his staff, and that the demons continued to work on his plans for many years after, not knowing that he was dead and that the power of the ring was now unmanned. At length a snake curled about the staff and it snapped and then the demons scattered.

The ring is thought to have been placed in the Holy of Holies in the Ark of the Covenant itself and never captured. A later magician went to rescue it when the soldiers of Titus were destroying the temple. He saw it and touched it, but then fainted and was carried to a strange land where a voice told him that the ring had been taken back to Heaven.

CHAPTER THIRTEEN

ORIENTAL MYTHS

Tibet's epic hero, Gesar of Ling, was a warrior, magician, smith and king who ruled the greatest kingdom in Tibet. The Gesar epic is recorded in many versions, but in its entirety is traditionally recited morning and afternoon by the folk singers of Tibet for forty-two days. The multi-skilled hero Gesar becomes the King of Ling by virtue of many feats of heroism and magic. His confirmation as king comes when the supernatural guardians of the kingdom allow him entry into a crystal mountain where the Treasures of Ling are kept.

As the King of Ling, Gesar takes possession of the great hall's countless treasures. Without doubt, the most important is the emblematic throne of the realm on which rests a huge gold mandala ring that is known as the 'Life of Ling' with a crystal vessel at its centre, from which flow the shining 'waters of immortality'.

Gesar's early life was not an easy one. Although born a royal prince, while he is still a child his parents are slain by Kurkar, the evil sorcerer and King of Hor. The orphaned Gesar is found in a heap of rubbish and adopted by a poor smith who raises him as an apprentice. Under the adopted name of Chori, he survives many attempts by sorcerers to kill him. He becomes an extraordinary alchemist by combining his skills as a smith with his inherited powers of sorcery. He creates many wonders in his smithy for his master, but for himself he forges an unbreakable sword from celestial (meteoric) iron.

Gesar prepares himself for his ultimate duel with his great enemy the King of

Hor. However, he knows that Kurkar cannot be slain until a huge iron mandala ring or talisman which is kept in the palace treasury is destroyed. This huge iron talisman contains the 'life' or 'soul' of Kurkar and all his ancestors.

The poet tells us: 'This sacred iron had been venerated for many centuries and in it reposed the vital essence of the dynasty of the Kings of Hor.' While the evil Kurkar himself says: 'It is the "life" of my ancestors. Sometimes sounds come from it, at other times it speaks.'

Gesar tricks the King of Hor into allowing him access to the iron talisman. However, it is believed Kurkar is safe because the iron cannot be melted or forged by any known means. The fire of the furnace does not even redden the sacred iron. Gesar is warned by the master smith: 'It is folly to think that it will let itself be forged.'

Gesar is no ordinary smith, and accepts the challenge. He summons his supernatural brothers and a multitude of spirits who manage to build a huge furnace and fill it with 'coal piled high as mountains'. This results in an inferno that is sufficient to forge the iron mandala. Gesar and his supernatural brothers strike the iron mandala with hammer blows that sound like thunder. At last the iron 'life' of the Kings of Hor is broken, though we are told 'the three worlds shook' with its destruction.

Once this is achieved, Gesar of Ling puts on his glittering armour and takes up his sword of celestial iron. In all his shining glory, Gesar appears before the evil King of Hor. Gesar declares his true identity to Kurkar and his mission of vengeance. Then, with a single stroke, Gesar of Ling cuts off the sorcerer's head.

In Tolkien's *The Lord of the Rings*, his evil Sauron the Ring Lord shares many characteristics with both Gesar of Ling and Kurkar of Hor. Like Gesar of Ling,

Sauron is both a supernaturally gifted smith capable of creating unmatched wonders upon his forge, and a magician capable of terrifying acts of sorcery. Both have mountain strongholds and both must keep safe the golden rings by whose powers they rule their kingdoms.

At this point the comparison between Gesar of Ling and Sauron of Mordor largely ceases. Gesar becomes an avenging angel of light; while Sauron the Dark Lord is much more closely allied to the values of the evil King of Hor. Kurkar – like both Gesar and Sauron – also has a ring or talisman that must be kept safe and by whose power he rules his kingdom. However, Kurkar's iron talisman is much more like Sauron's One Ring because both are inherently evil, and the sorcerers' lives depend on the survival of the rings. Kurkar's iron ring of Hor also shares the One Ring's characteristic of being almost indestructible. Normal fires do not even cause the metal in them to redden. Both require supernatural fires of volcanic intensity to melt them down.

The destruction of Kurkar's iron ring of Hor in Gesar's volcanic forge-room causes a cataclysm in which 'the three worlds shook.' Not to be outdone, this is matched by the climax of *The Lord of the Rings* when the destruction of Sauron's One Ring in Mount Doom's volcanic forge-room causes a comparable cataclysm in which 'the earth shook, the plain heaved and cracked, and... the skies burst into thunder seared with lightning.'

The Tibetan epic of Gesar of Ling – with its gold and iron mandala rings – is very obviously rooted in the ancient alchemical traditions. Alchemy combined the knowledge of the smith/smelter/miner with the supernatural powers of the magician/sorcerer/shaman. Gesar is a warrior-king who is both a smith and a magician. To such a hero, all things are possible. He assumes many forms, creates invulnerable weapons, conjures up phantom armies, and creates wealth and prosperity for his people.

In Asian myth and history, the connection between alchemy or metallurgy and the power of kings and heroes is often more obviously stated than it is in Europe. Tradition insists, for instance, that the great historic Mongol conqueror, Genghis Khan, was descended from a family of smiths. So too was the legendary Tartar hero Kok Chan who possessed a ring that – like Sauron's One Ring – hugely increased his already formidable powers.

Legends telling of heroes or villains possessing external souls that are kept hidden within objects outside the body are found in many cultures throughout the world. The legends spring from a number of sources. However, when the soul is kept in a metal object or a ring, one can be certain that the source of the legend is the magician-smith tradition of alchemy.

The epic events of Gesar's life demonstrate the ancient alchemical belief that not only can individual souls or lives be kept in a ring or talisman, but so can the souls or lives of entire dynasties and whole nations. This certainly parallels Tolkien's epic adventure where Sauron the Dark Lord's entire evil empire collapses with the One Ring's destruction.

This idea is suggested or implied in European ring quest epics like the Volsunga Saga and the Nibelungenlied, but the point is more often made explicitly in Asian epic tales. Perhaps this is because eastern religions or philosophies, such as Buddhism, are not in conflict with their shamanistic and alchemical traditions. Nor do they appear to have the Christian Church's need to vilify or eliminate these traditions.

Throughout Asia, the connection between the magician and the smith is absolute. In Siberia, the Buriat people divide smiths into two categories, black smiths and white smiths. This is exactly how they divide their shamans or magicians. Both black smiths and black magicians are feared because they are capable of capturing and destroying people's souls. Several Asian tribal peoples still maintain the belief that 'the sorcerer and the smith come from the same nest.' Both the smith and the magician are given the honoured title 'master of fire'.

This magician-smith tradition of northern Asia extended into northern Europe. Its strongest manifestation is probably found in the mythology of the Finno-Urgic people of Finland and Estonia. In origin, these were a nomadic Asiatic people who migrated west to the Baltic Sea. Racially and linguistically, they are unrelated to any other European race.

The supreme manifestation of their culture is the national epic of Finland, known as the Kalevala. (The Estonians have a variant of this tradition called the Kalevipoeg.) Tolkien read the epic as a student and immediately fell in love with the tale and the language. In his letters, he frequently acknowledges the Kalevala's influence, stating that it was 'the original germ of *The Silmarillion*.'

Tolkien also acknowledged that his Elvish language of Quenya (which he saw as a kind of 'Elf Latin') was linguistically styled on Finnish, in the same way that Sindarin or Grey Elvish was styled on Welsh.

It is possible that the Silmaril jewels of *The Silmarillion* were Tolkien's version of the Sampo, the mysterious treasure pursued by the heroes of the Kalevala.

Just what the Sampo is cannot really be determined. However, we are told it was an object of great and sacred value forged by the master smith Ilmarinen, a gift that is stolen and pursued, broken and lost (although surviving in fragments). This is not unlike the fate of the Silmarils – although descriptions of the forging of the Sampo suggest it is unlikely to be a jewel.

There is also a strong suggestion that Tolkien's hero Túrin Turambar in *The Silmarillion* is largely based on the Kalevala's cursed hero Kullervo. There are a few other similarities, for instance the names: Ilmatar and Ilmo from the Kalevala are similar to Ilúvatar and Ulmo from *The Silmarillion*. However, any detailed examination of the Kalevala demonstrates the truth in Tolkien's statement that it is only 'the original germ' of inspiration, not the model for *The Silmarillion*. By and large they are only incidentally comparable epics.

The mythology of the Orient has innumerable legends dealing with magic rings. In the Arabic world the use of magicians' rings of power was considered even more common than it was in the West. That wonderful anthology of eastern legends, *One Thousand and One Arabian Nights*, contains many tales involving magical rings. The most famous of these is the story of Aladdin's Magical Lamp. In the original story, we find that the genie of Aladdin's ring is far stronger and more useful than the genie of his lamp. The genie of his lamp gets him into no end of trouble, while the genie of the ring saves his life three times.

In India, the ring is often used as a symbol for the recognition of divinity in mortals. Among the many ring legends of this kind is one known as 'The Bodhisattva's Ring'. In this tale, the son of Brahmadatta, the King of Benares, is raised secretly as an untouchable stick-gatherer. The untouchable mother and child are brought to the throne-room. Recognition comes only when his mother throws the child into the air. Bearing a ruby ring in his hand, the child does not fall to the floor, but levitates in the air. The king accepts the child as his true heir and an incarnation of the Buddha.

In India, the quest for the ring can be almost entirely spiritual in nature. This is related to the Indian Vedic tradition which teaches that the 'ring of fire' burns away all ignorance and illusion. The pilgrim or warrior who passes through its flames attains a mystical state of perfect peace. This is like the Buddhist meditational state of Satori. This is the ring of fire at the centre of the universe and the Chidambaram, 'the centre of the universe which is within the heart.' It is an eternal place without time, where the true state of the soul may be observed and will grow to perfect wisdom.

To some degree, this Vedic ring of fire is comparable to the enchanted ring of fire which Sigurd the Volsung rode through to make his way to his Valkyrie bride. It is also comparable to the Elven rings of enchantment that protected the hidden Elf kingdoms of Lothlórien and Doriath from evil and the march of time. Then too there is its evil opposite, the satanic fiery ring that burned round the evil Eye of Sauron and preserved his damned spirit from mortal death.

The ancient histories of China tell how the monarchs of China wore rings that were unlike the rings of the West. For the alchemists of China believed that jade was the purest and most sacred substance, and the greatest value was placed on that hard stone. Their ruler's ring was not of gold or of some gem, but was a simple stone ring made from a unique blue jade. This was the sign of the power and glory of those omnipotent emperors through nearly four thousand years.

This blue jade ring was known as the Sky Ring of the Shang Dynasty, and the fate of this ring was bound up with the fate of China. There is one ancient tale concerning one of the Emperors who failed to uphold its tradition and suffered through the curse of the ring.

Chow Hsin was the thirtieth and last of the Shang emperors. He was corrupt, greedy, cruel and foolish; and he should not rightly have had the throne. Chow Hsin had none of the wisdom or divine balance of the Shang rulers. He abused his power. He indulged only in pleasure and ostentation, and he did not possess the one true ring of blue jade called the Sky Ring of Shang.

Chow Hsin's father, the Emperor Ti-yuh, had an older son called Khi who was born when the empress was still only his favourite concubine. Khi was modest, learned and pious. His father named him his heir and, in a secret ceremony on his death-bed, handed him the Sky Ring of blue jade that was the sacred sign of the Shangs.

But on the Emperor Ti-yuh's death, the ambitious Chow Hsin claimed that his brother Khi had no right to the throne, being born out of wedlock, and Chow usurped it. Thereafter Chow Hsin ruled the empire, but was always jealous and bitter of Khi and plotted against him. Khi retired to his estates in Wei and some power protected him from all attempts on his life and property.

The Shu Ching (Book of History) tells how, until the reign of this corrupt king, the power and wisdom of the Shangs were unmatched. For six centuries, the Shang Dynasty ruled China, and in that time the peoples prospered as never before. In their beginning the Shangs were jade-smiths who brought forth such beautiful dreaming forms from the incredibly hard stone that they became praised and worshipped by all people. For jade is the most sacred of substances in the world: the sons of Heaven feed upon jade, and Heaven itself has five jade mountains and four jade seas. Jade is a heavenly deputy: a bridge between mortals and the realm beyond.

There were nine colours of jade, of which blue jade was the rarest and most cherished, for upon Earth there was only the one blue stone that had fallen from Heaven. This one true jade of Heaven was in the hands of the Shang smiths, and so too was the K'ung Wu, the magic knife that cut jade like wax. These two great gifts were granted the Shangs by a magician who dwelt in the White Mountains of the west, beyond the inland sea. Thus the Shangs had possession and mastery of jade, and this gave them the wisdom of balance between heaven and earth. With the K'ung Wu they cut from the blue jade of Heaven the sacred Sky Ring of Shang. In each year of the Shangs' rule there were observed the Sky Ring ceremonies; the sacrifice to Heaven of calves, silks and rice. To their people the Shangs brought many arts that raised them above all others: writing, astronomy, divination, the use of money, the lunar calendar, the forging of bronze. So long as the Sky Ring passed from the father to the first son the empire seemed blessed. For with the ring the emperor could achieve harmony between Heaven and Earth.

But with the rule of Chow Hsin a great imbalance came to the empire. The ceremonies of the ring were abolished; the wisdom of the ring was lost. Chow oppressed his people and gathered to himself great wealth whilst enjoying many decadent and hedonistic pleasures.

It is said Chow Hsin had concubines beyond number, but always he desired more. On hearing of the beauty of Ta Chi, a princess of a neighbouring kingdom, he did not hesitate to demand her. When he was refused, he did not hesitate to lead his people into a bloody and disastrous war. At great price he won the pearl of that blameless kingdom, and with cruel torture he put to death Ta Chi's father, mother and brothers.

The cruel Chow Hsin found this woman to be fair indeed. Her face was as the white full moon and her beauty outshone that of Chow's other concubines as the moon outshines the stars. He proclaimed her the most beautiful woman in the world, but some believed that the lovely Ta Chi had bewitched the Emperor so that she might find some way to avenge the slaughter of her family.

Although the people of the empire had already suffered grievously in war because of the charms of this princess, Chow Hsin commanded that they must build a palace befitting her beauty. This was to be the Deer Tower (the 'Luhtae'), the greatest building in the world. It stood like a sheer mountain looming above the city of Po. It was half a mile long and had thousands of rooms. Its doors were set with jades and gems and its great chambers were fitted with bronze vessels, teak furnishings, and ornaments of ivory and gold. To this vain purpose, Chow Hsin enslaved all his people for seven long years and impoverished the nation. Neglecting all other duties of his high office, he allowed the land to fall into ruin. There was famine and plague, and Chow Hsin even failed to maintain the power of the armies that had allowed the Shangs to dwell in peace for so long.

On the borders of the empire the warlord Wan Wang, the Duke of Chow, looked upon the Shang lands with concern and dismay. Troubled by what he saw, he consulted the oracles of bone for divine guidance. He raised an army of chariots, cavalry and foot-soldiers and, after receiving a favourable sign from the oracles, he went to war. With great ceremony Wan Wang crossed the Huang River and entered into the empire of the Shangs unchallenged.

Now Chow Hsin betrayed his people for the last time. He had the keeper of the treasury bring all that remained in the vaults of the nation and all the ancient Imperial Jades of the Shangs to him. Then he climbed to the top of the Deer Tower and set fire to himself and all the wealth of the empire. His people were left with nothing and all their labour of seven years was destroyed.

Wan Wang observed the ceremonies of the time. Thus, as conqueror, he rode to the ruins of the Deer Tower and shot three arrows from his chariot. He then climbed out and decapitated Chow Hsin's charred body with his yellow axe. The head was impaled upon his great white standard. Next Wan Wang had Ta Chi, the concubine, brought before him and strangled. Again he fired three arrows and then decapitated her with his black axe. The adorned head was impaled on his small white standard. Now he was conqueror but, with all the Imperial Jades ruined by fire, he could not be emperor and father to the people.

Then came Khi to Wan Wang's camp, making the traditional gestures of surrender and self-sacrifice. He came naked to the waist, with his hands bound and drawing an empty coffin behind him. In his mouth he held the sacred Sky Ring of Shang. Wan Wang received Khi before his field pavilion. He raised Khi up with his own hands, untied his wrists and accepted from him the ring of blue jade. Mercifully, Wan Wang burned the coffin instead of Khi and returned him to his estates in Wei.

Now that Wan Wang was emperor he restored his empire and reinstituted the ring sacrifices. Peace and prosperity returned to the land. The mastery of jade

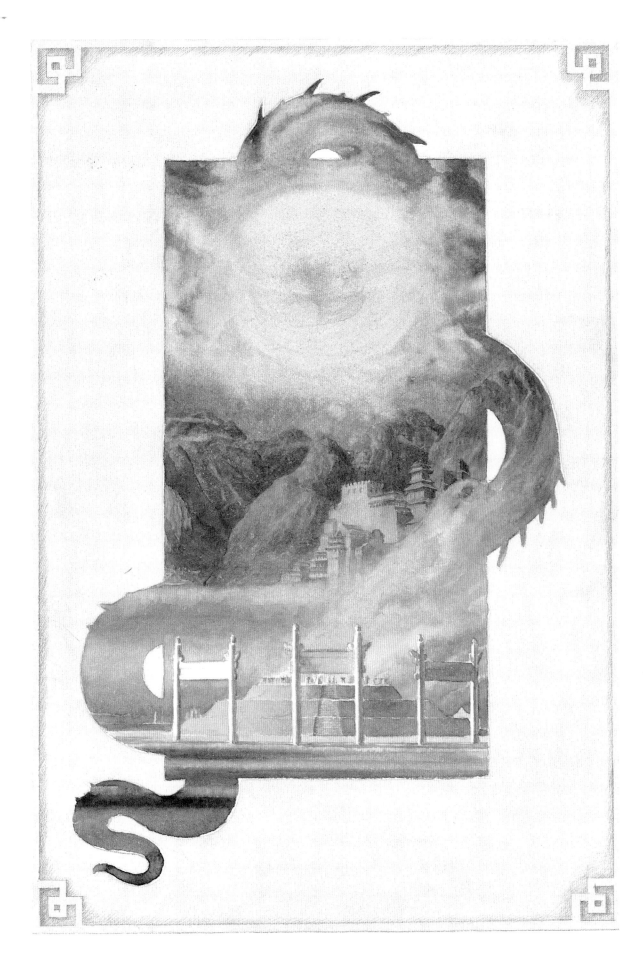

and bronze was raised to new heights and the arts brought by the Shangs thrived once again.

So began the Chow Dynasty of nine centuries. Wan Wang used the Sky Ring of the one true jade of Heaven as it was intended. Heaven and Earth were in harmony once more.

CHAPTER FOURTEEN

THE ALCHEMIST'S RING

The symbol for the alchemist was a gold ring in the form of a serpent swallowing its own tail. This serpent ring is the Ouroboros, meaning 'tail-biter', a symbol for eternity that is found in a score of mythologies. In many cultures we find in the great serpent the first form to emerge from chaos; it then encircles the void and creates time and space by forming a ring, becoming the Ouroboros and grasping its own tail. We see this celestial serpent ring in the Babylonian serpent called Eä, the Greek Ophion, the Hindu Sheshna, the Chinese Naga, and the Norse Jormangand.

The ring was a symbol of the alchemist's profession and a vision of the alchemist's quest. This was a ring very like that seen in a vision by the seventeenth-century metaphysical poet, Henry Vaughan, in his poem 'The World':

> I saw Eternity the other night
> Like a great Ring of pure and endless light,
> All calm, as it was bright,
> And round beneath it, Time in hours, days, years
> Driv'n by the spheres...

To the alchemist, the ring shaped like, or engraved with, the 'eternal' serpent and made of 'immortal' gold was the symbol for universal knowledge. It was – one might say – the 'One Ring' by which all others are ruled.

The power of the alchemist traditionally evolved through a combination of natural science and supernatural wisdom which are embodied in the crafts of the shaman (or magician) and the smith. These are derived from the symbols and mysteries of metallurgy, and are ultimately emblematic of the physical and spiritual mastery of fire.

Traditionally, the alchemist – like the magician and the smith – is given the title 'master of fire'. The smith's mastery of fire is obvious enough in his forging of metals. The magician – from the most obscure tribal shaman to Wizards like Gandalf – handles fire and flame as a demonstration of mastery of spiritual power. Indeed, in many cultures the magicians, fakirs and shaman are traditionally renowned for walking on hot coals and spitting fire. The alchemist employs both physical and spiritual fire to transform the natural world.

In Tolkien's world of *The Lord of the Rings*, we have the ultimate evil alchemist in the form of Sauron, the Ring Lord. Sauron is both a magician (or sorcerer) and a smith who forges the supernatural One Ring of Power. He has the perfect evil alchemist's pedigree. He was originally a good fire spirit apprenticed to the Valarian god, Aulë the Smith. He betrayed his master and became the disciple of Melkor the Dark Sorcerer. Typically, Sauron's means of conquest are not confined to force of arms. Through a combination of his skills as a sorcerer and a smith, he creates the ultimate weapon in his One Ring of Power.

We are told that the mortal Easterlings and Southrons saw Sauron as both king and god and feared him, for he surrounded his abode with fire. Sauron built the Dark Tower of Mordor near the fiery volcano of Mount Doom. The volcanic

'Cracks of Doom' brought him near 'the heart of the earth in his sorceries and in his forging' where in the 'midst of the Land of Mordor he had fashioned the One Ring.'

Many races fell quickly and easily under the spell of the One Ring, but those enemies of Sauron who could not be immediately enslaved were resilient chiefly because they too possessed elements of alchemical power. These were the Noldor Elves, the Dwarves, and the Númenóreans.

The greatest of these were the Noldor Elves who were already gifted with 'Elven magic' before they became the students and disciples of Aulë the Smith. (In Tolkien's original drafts the Noldor were actually called the Gnomes, from the Greek 'Ge-nomos' meaning 'earth-dweller'; while Noldor is Elvish for 'knowledge'; just as Gnostic – the alchemical sect – is from the Greek 'Gnosis' meaning 'knowledge'.) Greatest of the Noldor Elves was Fëanor (meaning 'spirit of fire'), who in *The Silmarillion* combined Elvish spells and smith's skills to forge the famous Silmarils. These are the 'jewels of light' stolen by Sauron's master, Melkor the Lord of Darkness, and over which the wars of the First Age were fought. Fëanor's grandson was the Noldor prince Celebrimbor, the Lord of the Elven-smiths of Eregion, who forged the Rings of Power, over which the wars of the Second and Third Ages were fought.

The Dwarves were also tough opponents, for they were a race who were shaped by Aulë the Smith. They were resilient to fire both physical and sorcerous. They were a stubborn race who marked their weapons and armour with Dwarf runes and spells. The greatest of the Dwarves was Telchar the Smith whose weapons were blessed with such powers that one (the knife called Angrist) was used to cut a Silmaril from Melkor's (Morgoth's) iron crown; and another (the sword Narsil) was used to cut the One Ring from Sauron's hand.

The Númenóreans and their Dúnedain descendants on Middle-earth learned their alchemical skills from the Noldor Elves and the Dwarves; and in some creations even outdid their masters. So, as the Dúnedain of the North and the Men of Gondor were the surviving descendants of these great people, and the chief inheritors of ancient wisdom which gave them the power to resist evil temptation, these people were seen by Sauron as the chief obstacles to his dominion of Middle-earth.

However, there were also the Istari or Wizards who were sent by the Valar to Middle-earth as adversaries of Sauron the Ring Lord. Yet, of the five Wizards who came, only Gandalf was able to stand against Sauron uncorrupted. For it was Gandalf wearing Narya – the Elf 'ring of fire' – who best understood the alchemical nature of the conflict with Sauron. It was Gandalf who discovered and translated the 'secret language' of the One Ring which was 'written in fire'.

149

Gandalf's Elf ring and Sauron's One Ring were both symbolic of the control of alchemical fire, but alchemical fire of different types. The evil alchemy that made the One Ring commanded the dark satanic fire out of the bowels of the earth. This power transformed the material world – or at least gave that illusion, and the accompanying illusion of worldly power.

The good alchemy of Gandalf's Elf ring commanded the celestial fire of the spirit. When the Elf ring Narya is given to Gandalf by Círdan, the Shipwright says: 'Take this ring, Master ... this is the Ring of Fire, and with it you may rekindle the hearts in a world that grows chill.' This 'good' alchemical fire has no power over the material world. However, the fire of the spirit does have the power to impassion and uplift the soul because ultimately its source is the sacred 'Flame Imperishable' of Eru the One – the Supreme Being who gave all things life.

We see this duel between the two kinds of alchemical fire vividly illustrated in Gandalf's battle with Sauron's mightiest demon – the Balrog of Moria – on the Bridge of Khazad-dûm. In Gandalf's challenge to the Balrog, we see the clear distinction between the two types of alchemical fire. Gandalf tells the monster: 'I am a servant of the Secret Fire, wielder of the flame of Anor. You cannot pass. The dark fire will not avail you, flame of Udûn. Go back to the Shadow! You cannot pass.'

This head-on conflict, of course, led to mutual destruction. Gandalf foresaw this, but made the sacrifice because no other way was possible. However, Gandalf also understood that ultimately the only way to defeat Sauron and his evil One Ring was not to attempt to overthrow him or to seize its power, but to undo the alchemical process by which the Ring of Power was made. Once Gandalf understood the 'language of the ring', he knew that only by reversing the alchemical process could Sauron be defeated. Just as common folklore tells us one can undo a spell by reciting it backwards, so Gandalf understood that the only way the One Ring could be destroyed was to reverse the process by which it was made. This was the reason for *The Lord of the Rings*' 'backward' ring quest. The One Ring had to be taken back to the crucible where it was made. Only there in the fiery furnace of the 'Cracks of Doom' where it was forged could the One Ring be unmade – and Sauron's power destroyed.

In its creation, Sauron's One Ring was the ultimate heresy against the alchemical tradition. It was the evil opposite of the Ouroboros or serpent ring of the alchemist. When Sauron came to the Elven-smiths of Middle-earth and persuaded them to forge the other Rings of Power, he came in disguise as Annatar, 'giver of gifts'. He appeared as a benevolent alchemist very like the Greek hero Prometheus. In fact, he was the exact opposite. Prometheus's ring marked the saviour who enslaved himself and gave mortals freedom, knowledge and life. Sauron's ring marked the tyrant who enslaved the world and gave mortals bondage, ignorance and death.

When considering the alchemist tradition of the serpent ring, the Ouroboros, it is essential to recognize that it was also the symbol of the early Christian religion and philosophy known as Gnosticism. In its doctrines, Jesus tells the Virgin Mary: 'The Outer darkness is a great serpent, the tail of which is in its mouth, and it is outside the whole world, and surroundeth the whole world.' Gnosticism also taught that the serpent and the Christ were interchangeable figures, and that both were saviours or 'redeemers'.

By the first century AD, Gnostic religion and Western alchemical doctrine were largely indistinguishable. This eventually proved to be unfortunate for the older tradition of alchemy. Gnosticism became such a successful competitor for converts that St John and St Paul constantly railed against (and shamelessly libelled) its missionaries and saints. Later Christians so ruthlessly suppressed Gnostic teachings that the possession of an Ouroboros ring was sufficient grounds for the charge of heresy and sorcery. The result was that even after the virtual extermination of Gnosticism by the sixth century, Christian fanatics tended to view the alchemist's ring as a satanic relic.

If Tolkien's One Ring was an evil version of the Alchemist's Ring with its secret spell and language written in fire, what were the mysteries of the alchemist's rings all about? Naturally enough, in the hostile world of Christian suppression, the already obscure and symbolic language of alchemist and Gnostic became even more veiled and secretive. The ancient alchemical text by Hortulanus, the 'Rosarium Philosophorum', warns that such studies must be 'transmitted mystically as poetry uses fables and parables.'

A cornerstone of Western alchemical belief is the teaching of the third-century scholar and visionary, Zosimos of Panopolis. In 'The Visions of

151

Zosimos', we find the rituals and the actual process of the alchemical transmutation of metals. As always with alchemy a 'secret language' of coded symbols is used to describe these rituals and processes. (In one system of Taoist alchemy, we are told, for instance, that the tiger was the symbol for lead and the dragon the symbol for mercury. Obviously, however, different systems used different codes, and the 'keys' to these codes have usually been long lost in the sands of antiquity.)

Zosimos emphasizes the importance of understanding the 'secret words' of his vision. 'This introduction is the key which shall open to you the flowers of the discourse that is to follow, namely, investigation of the arts, of wisdom, of reason and understanding, the efficatious methods and revelations which throw light upon the secret words.' What is extraordinary is that the symbols and the narrative pattern of his 'Visions' add up to what is essentially a ring quest.

Zosimos of Panopolis's 'Visions' are a mystical dream-vision in which he finds himself manifest as pilgrim on a long and perilous journey: 'I followed the road alone ... I again went astray, not knowing my way, and I stopped in despair. And again, as it seemed, I saw an old man whitened by years ... And I urged him: "Show me the right way."'

At last Zosimos as the dream hero comes to a circular temple, which itself has the shape of a huge stone ring. He describes it as cut 'from a single stone with neither end nor beginning in its construction'.

There the hero is instructed to '... take a sword in your hand; then seek the entrance, for narrow is the place where the opening is. A dragon lies at the entrance, guarding the temple. Lay hold of him; immolate him first; ... then, laying the limbs together with the bones at the entrance of the temple, make a step of them, mount thereon, and enter, and you will find what you seek.'

In Zosimos's vision, we have the typical questing hero, aided by an ancient adviser and guide (aka Gandalf, Merlin, Odin) who tells him what road to take and how with a sacred sword he may overcome the guardian serpent at the door to the temple (which is itself a ring) where the object of his quest may be found.

However, there are a number of very special aspects to Zosimos's 'Visions'. For Zosimos's dream-vision did not actually begin with the hero embarking on his quest, as most traditional stories might. Strangely enough, the 'Visions' actually begin with Zosimos seeing through the eyes of the dragon or Ouroboros, as he is (willingly) being slaughtered by the hero whom he calls 'the sacrificer'.

So Zosimos's 'Visions' begin: 'And as I spoke thus I fell asleep, and I saw the sacrificer standing before me ... who overpowered me, and pierced me through with the sword, and dismembered me in accordance with the rule of harmony.'

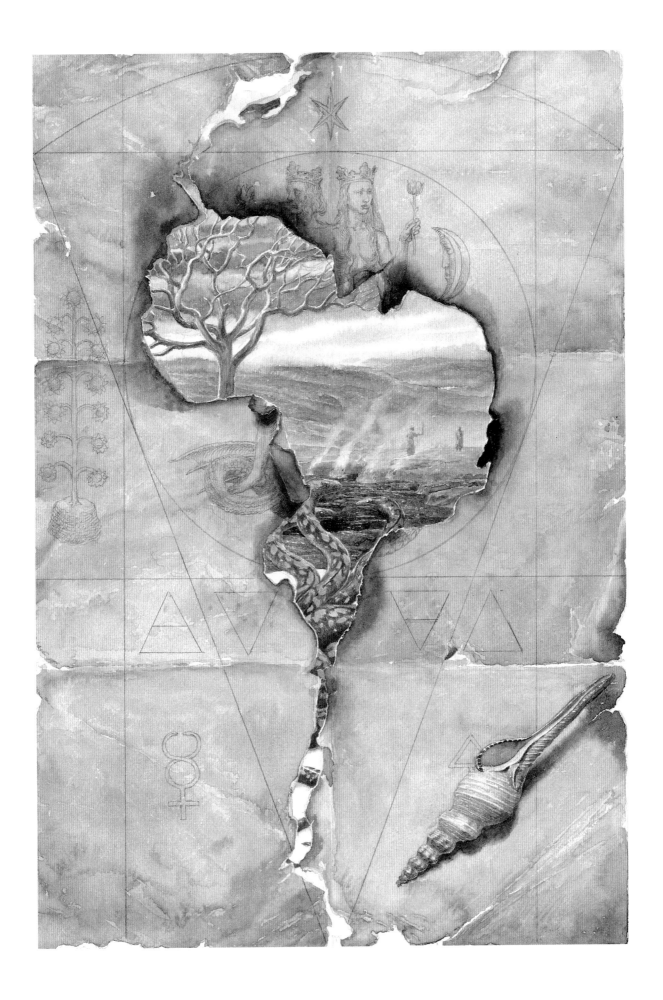

(And so one is here reminded that, to the Gnostic, both the serpent and the Christ are voluntary sacrificial victims, and 'redeemers'.)

One of the most intense investigations into alchemical studies and symbols in the twentieth century was conducted by one of the founders of modern psychology, Carl Jung. Upon reading and studying the works of Zosimos, and the 'Visions' in particular, Jung wrote: 'Zosimos is speaking here in the conscious language of his art, and expresses himself in terms that are obviously familiar to his reader.'

The quest dream was consciously written by Zosimos both to convey the alchemical belief in the transmutation of metals, and the belief in the transmutation of the spirit. In terms of Jung's modern psychology, this quest dream was about integrating conflicting aspects of human personality and life harmony.

> Once again the universal struggle of the hero with the dragon is enacted, and each time at its victorious conclusion the sun rises: consciousness dawns, and it is perceived that the transformation process is taking place inside the (ring-shaped) temple.

> It is in truth the inner man, who passes through the stages that transform copper into silver and silver into gold, and who thus undergoes a gradual enhancement of value ... It sounds very strange to modern ears that the inner man and his spiritual growth should be symbolized by metals. But the historical facts cannot be doubted, nor is the idea peculiar to alchemy.

Carl Jung also observed the significance of the alchemist's ring in the 'circular thinking' of the dream-vision and the dreamer's identification with both the hero and his victim, the serpent. Jung concluded that the hero is as much the Ouroboros as the serpent 'whose circular form is suggested by the shape of the temple, which has neither beginning nor end in its construction.' Zosimos's visions are very like the riddle engraved on a famous ring of Mary Queen of Scots, which read: 'In my beginning is my end.'

What is Zosimos's dream quest about? Carl Jung saw it in psychological terms as the integration of the psyche. The alchemists saw the stated goal of attempting to transmute base metals into pure gold as a material manifestation of a spiritual quest in the transformation of the mortal soul into a pure immortal spirit.

Zosimos's pilgrim enters the ring-shaped temple which is the crucible wherein base metals are transformed into 'pure alchemist's gold', which is called the

'Spirit of Mercurius'. Then we are told about the nature of the pure alchemical spirit: 'Mercurius has the circular nature of the Ouroboros, hence he is symbolized by the circulus simplex of which he is at the same time the centre. He can therefore say of himself: "I am One and at the same time Many in myself."'

The simplicity and sophistication of this statement is remarkable, both in terms of Jung's psychology, and what might amount to a mystic vision of the universe. In Mercurius the Ouroboros which is the alchemist's ring we are given the simplest symbol of eternity, and therefore the essential image of God.

Jung's discovery of alchemy was one of the greatest intellectual adventures of his life. He gradually came to believe that he 'had stumbled upon the historical counterpart of the psychology of the unconscious.' In alchemy and myths he saw symbols of a subconscious, universal language – a 'secret language' of the psyche which the unconscious understood, even if the mind did not. He even adopted the alchemist's Ouroboros as the symbol for his own psychiatric research institute.

However, to go back to the business of the 'language of the ring', it is interesting to look at this idea historically in relation to the many beliefs in the power of rings that have permeated our culture. An important example was one of the major historical figures in alchemy and Gnosticism, Apollonius of Tyana. Apollonius was a learned man who in the first century AD had been initiated into the famous Pythagorean cult mysteries of Greece, along with some of the wisest men of his age. After many years of study, he then observed five years of silence and wandered into the lands of the Indian Brahmans where he gained even greater knowledge and wisdom. There he is said to have received seven rings as a gift from the Brahman master and Indian prince, Iarchus. Each ring was marked with a different stone, and Apollonius wore them one by one in order of the days of the week, 'for it is said that he revered them as divine, so that he changed them each day and made them partakers of his greatest secrets.'

Historical evidence suggests Apollonius was a blamelessly compassionate scholar who brought healing and knowledge to many during his lifetime. Yet he became the victim of fifteen centuries of Christian attack. So vilified was he in Christian propaganda that his ring consultations began to sound rather like Tolkien's evil character Gollum, who insanely talked to his 'precious' evil ring. Tolkien tells us that the One Ring seemed to possess Gollum more than Gollum possessed the ring, and that 'he talked to it, even when it was not with him.'

What is behind all this business of 'talking to rings'? Are these testimonies about people communing with spirits in rings total fabrications made up to condemn Christian heretics? Or was there some real basis for these strange accusations?

Let us look more closely at the case of Apollonius. I suggest that it is very likely that Apollonius of Tyana did 'consult' his rings as was rumoured. Furthermore, in a very real sense, those seven rings did in fact contain much of his secret knowledge. And as he was a renowned teacher, we are told – probably correctly – that when others came under his influence, they also acquired similar 'magic rings' which they too would consult in the manner of their master.

It is fairly obvious that Apollonius's famous 'Seven Rings' were a memory system of mystic knowledge not unlike that of the sixteenth-century Japanese system of the samurai master Miyamoto Musashi. The Japanese system is a guide to strategy and martial arts known as the 'Go Rin No Sho', or the 'Book

155

of Five Rings'. In the Japanese system, each ring is of a different element – Ring of Earth, Ring of Water, Ring of Fire, Ring of Wind, Ring of Darkness – and each ring teaches a different aspect of military strategy.

As the historical scholar Frances Yates has recorded in her book *The Art of Memory*, the primary and often sole means of teaching in ancient and medieval times was oral, and knowledge was retained by human memory alone. For even with the advent of literate scholars and hand-written books and records, it was not until the invention of the printing press that knowledge had any broad circulation outside of oral teaching traditions. For the majority of Europe's population up to the nineteenth century, it remained the primary means of learning.

Consequently, the first priority of all scholars or potential scholars was the acquisition of a system of memory by which knowledge acquired could be stored and retrieved when needed. Every teaching institution or sect had a system of some kind. These systems varied widely in shape and complexity. Most often, Frances Yates suggests, they took on an architectural form, such as massive temples with extensive grounds and gardens. Each part of the building represented a different category within which information about a different art or science would be stored. Within these larger systems were often smaller ones involving staircases, ladders, ropes and rings.

It is quite obvious that Apollonius taught an alchemist memory system that was a kind of 'ring oracle' or an intellectual's form of dactyliomancy. It was a memory system where each ring was a catalogue file to a library of gnostic and alchemical knowledge.

So, strangely enough, these recurring accusations of sorcery by consulting rings begin to make some sense. Also, the notion of learning a secret language of rings as a means of gaining wisdom and power has a rational explanation. Undoubtedly, the recitation of the meaning of each ring in order to retain it in the mind was a necessary means of maintaining the memory system. As a trained Pythagorean, Apollonius certainly already had at least one major memory system developed and in use; his 'Seven Rings' was probably a new additional system of his own invention.

The problem was that the early Christian opponents of Gnosticism were primarily fundamentalist and anti-intellectual in nature. Christian archbishops proudly burned ancient Greco-Roman libraries, closed universities and drove scholars into exile. Many scholars had to flee to Baghdad and other parts of the Moslem world. Indeed, if it had not been for the tolerance and intellectual enlightenment of the leaders of Islam at this time, much of the art, science and literature of the ancient Greco-Roman civilization would have been lost forever.

The madness and paranoia of fundamentalist Christianity emerged again and again throughout the Middle Ages and inevitably resulted in the persecution of anyone with intellectual pretensions who was not directly under the protection of the Church. Consequently, it is easy to see how charges about alchemists and other scholars 'speaking with devils' imprisoned in rings could gain currency. However, from such a simplistic point of view, any kind of memory system or recitation used to retain and pass on knowledge was suspect. By such absurd standards, it would not take much imagination to accuse pious Christians of 'speaking with devils' for their far less intellectually taxing habits of counting their rosaries or reciting the Stations of the Cross.

Alchemists and Gnostics were also known to have used another related but different 'oracle' of a meditational kind. This was 'ophiomancy' or an oracle of serpents, which was most highly developed by the Gnostic Ophite sect. All Gnostic sects used the Ouroboros ring as their symbol, but by the Ophites the serpent was especially regarded as the master of all knowledge and the father of all arts and sciences.

In fact, the prophetic system of ophiomancy is much older than Gnosticism. Throughout Hellenistic times, most oracles and centres of healing used ophiomancy as a prophetic and meditational technique. Harmless golden temple snakes were kept and were observed by pilgrims and priests in order to interpret or facilitate prophetic dreams.

Among some Ophite sects ophiomancy was transformed into a highly developed meditational technique for associative thought which allowed the enquiring mind free play. To simplistic Christian zealots, this was a clear example of snake worship and 'satanic practices'.

One wonders what those stern Church fathers would have made of the nineteenth-century scientist Friedrich August Kekulé. Kekulé knew a great deal about alchemy, and recorded how he once employed ophiomancy as a meditational technique which resulted in the single most important scientific discovery of his life.

In 1865, the greatest breakthrough in modern chemistry and in understanding the structure of matter came with the formulation of 'Kekulé's Theory'. It is claimed that three-quarters of modern chemistry is directly or indirectly the result of this theory.

Kekulé's own description of his discovery shows how he acknowledged and practised alchemical meditational techniques.

* * *

I was sitting, writing at my text-book; but the work did not progress; my thoughts were elsewhere. I turned my chair to the fire and dozed. Again the atoms were gambolling before my eyes. This time the smaller groups kept modestly in the background. My mental eye, rendered more acute by repeated visions of the kind, could now distinguish larger structures of manifold conformation; long rows, sometimes more closely fitted together; all twining and twisting in snake-like motion. But look! What was that? One of the snakes has seized hold of its own tail, and the form whirled mockingly before my eyes. As if by a flash of lightning I awoke; and this time also I spent the rest of the night in working out the consequences of the hypothesis.

Here we find the Ouroboros coming into its enigmatic, radiant own again across the centuries. The hypothesis that the Ouroboros suggested to Kekulé resulted in the discovery of the molecular structure of benzene. This was the breakthrough that gave chemistry the now accepted hypothesis that all organic nature is based on the structure of the carbon ring.

To the alchemist and the Gnostic, the Ouroboros serpent ring held the secret of life itself. In Kekulé's vision, we have a demonstration of how the alchemist's

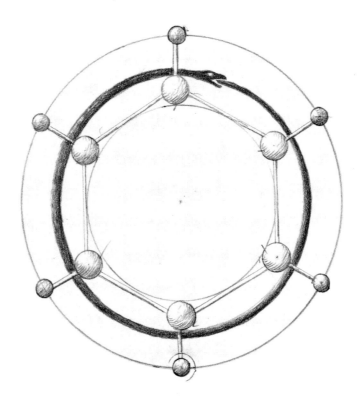

ring, if not delivering the actual 'secret of life', was certainly the means by which one of its secrets was revealed to us.

Looking at the tradition of the alchemist in the history of the ring, we can see in Sauron the Ring Lord something of the Christian world's dark vision of an evil alchemist using a 'ring of power' to destroy or enslave life. There are enough antique poison rings, and rings filled with scrolls upon which curses are written, for us to know that rings were sometimes used by sorcerers. There is no doubt that some practitioners of witchcraft actually did use rings for evil purposes; however, for the most part the ring lords of the 'true' alchemical tradition commanded and worshipped a ring of exactly the opposite nature.

CHAPTER FIFTEEN

WAGNER'S RING

Richard Wagner's first performance of *The Ring of the Nibelung* in 1876 has often been cited as the first great expression of the identity of the recently unified German nation. Certainly, Wagner saw art as a political as well as an aesthetic act, and with his *Ring* he was attempting to claim a mythological heritage and a national art. For Wagner, art and myth were linked. He believed that true art must arise from the primordial depths of a people's collective being, the 'Volk'. His *Ring* was a purposeful act of making a statement of German identity and claiming the root of that identity was to be found in the Germanic epic tradition of the ring quest myths.

Criticized as Wagner may be for his manipulations and distortions of Norse myth and medieval German literature, it was his genius which recognized the significance of the ring myth, and the importance of reclaiming it for his own time. Furthermore, one must recognize that Wagner's opera brilliantly conveys the huge spirit of this ancient tale on a truly epic scale. Just as the Volsunga Saga and The Nibelungenlied were interpretations of the quest appropriate to their times, so Wagner's *The Ring of the Nibelung* was true to the spirit of his time.

In the second half of the nineteenth century, there was an awakening and flowering of interest in the Teutonic mythologies in Europe, and the ring quest emerged as a major theme in European literature. It was William Morris who (with Eirikr Magnusson) gave the English the first full-blooded translation of the Volsunga Saga in 1870. He proclaimed the Icelandic epic the Iliad of northern Europe. Later, Morris followed this up with his own epic-length

161

poem, 'Sigurd the Volsung', which appeared in 1876, the same year as Wagner's *The Ring of the Nibelung* was first staged at Bayreuth.

The playwright and critic George Bernard Shaw saw Morris's 'Sigurd' as one of the most monumental poems of the century. Shaw also wrote what must be the most brilliantly eccentric examination of Wagner's opera in his 'The Perfect Wagnerite'. (Shaw saw *The Ring of the Nibelung* as an allegory about socialism: the Manchester working class being the hell-born, miserable dwarf-slaves of the evil dictatorial corporate stockholder Alberich!)

The Norwegian dramatist Henrik Ibsen adapted the Volsunga Saga in his early play *The Vikings at Helgeland*, and later used many of the same elements and themes in such mature works as *Peer Gynt*. During this period, the English poet, Matthew Arnold, wrote his 'Balder Dead'; while Andrew Lang, George MacDonald and Henry Wadsworth Longfellow were among the many who popularized Teutonic myth and legend in the English-speaking world. On the Continent, there was Christian Kebbel's trilogy *Die Nibelungen*, and that monumental and massively influential study *Teutonic Mythology* by Jacob Grimm.

However, of them all, it is Wagner's *The Ring of the Nibelung* that is the ring legend of the age. In this opera, we see all of what comes before: mythically, historically, spiritually. It was Wagner who, in the four parts of his opera cycle ('The Rhinegold', 'The Valkyrie', 'Siegfried', 'The Twilight of the Gods') reforged the ring for his time.

'The Rhinegold'

SCENE ONE

In the depths of a river, the three water nymphs – the Rhinemaidens – play and sing in the limpid green depths. These are the beautiful daughters of the Rhine River who are spied on by Alberich the Nibelung. The ugly Dwarf has made his way down into their watery realm where he lustfully and fruitlessly pursues the teasing nymphs. Enraged by their mocking, the Dwarf is suddenly overcome by a brilliant golden glow. Rays of sunlight catch on a gold pinnacle of rock which fills the murky river with shimmering gold light. The nymphs sing praises to this treasure, the Rhinegold, which is a stone that – if forged into a gold ring – would allow its master to become lord of the world. However, the Rhinegold can be taken and mastered only by one who is willing to curse love and renounce all love's pleasures. Since Alberich is too ugly to win love anyway, he will take power: he swears an oath renouncing love. The Nibelung then snatches the Rhinegold from the pinnacle and flees into the dark.

SCENE TWO

Dawn comes to a mountain height above the Rhine Valley where Wotan, the king of the gods, and his queen, Fricka, sleep. In the distance stands a magnificent castle with gleaming battlements, up on an impossibly high peak. Fricka wakes Wotan, and the god is filled with delight at the sight of the newly completed kingdom of the gods. This was a realm built by the brute force of giants, but conceived in Wotan's dreams. Unfortunately the price promised to the giants Fasolt and Fafner for building this kingdom was the hand of Fricka's sister, Freia, the goddess of youth. However, with Freia the gods will also lose the golden apples of immortality of which she is guardian, and without this fruit will soon grow old and die. When the giants come for their payment, Donner, the god of thunder, Froh, the god of spring, and Loge, the trickster god of fire, come to side with Wotan to defend Freia. But the bargain cannot be broken as Wotan has sworn to make payment upon his sacred spear of law. It is up to Loge to come up with an alternative payment. The giants agree: they will have the Ring of the Nibelung which Alberich has forged from the stolen Rhinegold, along with all the golden treasures he has amassed through its power. Loge also reveals that if the ring is not soon taken from Alberich, he will rule over all of them anyway. The giants take Freia as a hostage as Wotan and Loge descend into the bowels of the earth in search of the realm of Alberich the Nibelung.

SCENE THREE

The subterranean caverns of Nibelheim, the home of the Nibelung Dwarfs, are a vast stone labyrinth of tunnels and chambers. This is a dark and sinister world lit only by the red glow of furnace and forge. Here, Alberich the ring lord torments his enslaved brother Mime, who has just completed the forging of the magic helmet called Tarnhelm on Alberich's orders. Tarnhelm has the power to make the wearer invisible or change him into whatever form he wishes. It can also transport him to any place he wishes. Alberich places the Tarnhelm on his head and immediately vanishes. The invisible Alberich then cruelly kicks and beats Mime until he cries out for mercy. Delighted with his new toy, Alberich goes off to terrorize his other enslaved Dwarfs. Mime continues to bewail his enslavement, as the gods Wotan and Loge enter the cavern. Alberich soon returns, driving his treasure-bearing Dwarfs before him. They pile up a huge hoard of purest gold. Alberich contemptuously greets his guests, and arrogantly reveals how he will build up such vast wealth and power that he will eventually overthrow the gods and rule the world. Wotan can barely contain his anger, but crafty Loge flatters the Dwarf and asks him about the powers of Tarnhelm. Can it really transform him into any shape, he asks? Certainly, Alberich replies, and immediately becomes a huge dragon. Loge feigns fear and astonishment, but then suggests that it would surely be more impressive if the Dwarf could become something really small, like a toad. Alberich foolishly obliges and transforms himself into a tiny toad. Wotan immediately seizes the tiny toad, while Loge snatches up Tarnhelm. When Alberich resumes his usual shape, he is bound and dragged off as a captive.

SCENE FOUR

The bound Alberich is taken to the misty mountain height above the Rhine where the bargain with the giants was struck. In order to win his freedom, Alberich is forced to give up his hoard of gold, Tarnhelm, and his magic ring. The enraged Dwarf refuses, but finally everything is taken from him. Once the humiliated Alberich is released, he wrathfully places a curse of disaster and death on anyone who commands the ring. Soon after, all the gods gather with the giants, Fasolt and Fafner, and their hostage Freia. Fasolt is in love with Freia, but agrees to accept gold only if it completely hides her from his sight. The gods pile all the gold around her, but Fasolt can still see the sheen of her hair, so Loge gives up Tarnhelm to cover it. She seems entirely covered, but Fasolt cries out that he can still see the star-like glint of her eye. The giants demand the ring to seal the crack, but Wotan is enthralled by the ring's power and will not give it up. Loge meanwhile claims it for its rightful owners, the Rhinemaidens. In the midst of the quarrel, the earth splits open and Erda, goddess of the earth, arises out of the ground. She is the spirit of the world and the prophet of the gods. She commands Wotan to surrender the ring or the gods and all their realm will be doomed. Almost immediately the curse of the ring strikes when the giants quarrel over its possession. Fafner brutally murders Fasolt and takes both the ring and the treasure. After Fafner's departure, Donner walks into the mountain mists where the thunder of his hammer is heard and flashes of lightning are seen as he forges a rainbow bridge. It arches through the air and leads up to the great castle of the gods, which Wotan now names Valhalla. Wotan leads the godly procession over the rainbow bridge to Valhalla, while far below the Rhinemaidens cry out for the loss of their gold.

'The Valkyrie'

ACT ONE, SCENE ONE

A storm is raging, and the hero Siegmund the Walsung enters the great hall of the warrior-chieftain Hunding. In the middle of the dwelling is the trunk of a huge ash tree whose limbs support the roof. He is wounded and exhausted from pursuit by enemies through the forest. He collapses on a bearskin before the fire in the enormous stone hearth. Hunding's wife Sieglinde enters the house and, seeing the now unconscious Siegmund, takes pity on him and revives him. Instantly, there is a powerful attraction between the two.

SCENE TWO

Hunding arrives home and reluctantly offers shelter and food to Siegmund. When he asks Siegmund his name, the youth gives his outlaw name, Wehwalt the Wolfing. His name means 'Woeful': his father Wolfe, his mother and his twin sister were all slain or lost to him. As he describes his latest disasters, it is soon revealed that his enemies are Hunding's kinsmen. Hunding tells his guest he is safe for the night, but in the morning he must find a weapon and they will duel to the death.

SCENE THREE

Alone in the great hall, Siegmund is soon joined by Sieglinde, who has given Hunding a sleeping-potion. Sieglinde tells Siegmund how she had been orphaned as a child, and as a captive was given as a reluctant bride to Hunding. But to the wedding came a stranger: an old man dressed all in grey with a slouch hat and a single glittering eye. That old man brought a bright sword and drove it into the mighty ash tree that holds up the roof of Hunding's house. Many heroes since that time have tried to draw it out, but none could do it. When Sieglinde confesses her unhappiness, Siegmund swears his love for her and promises to free her from her forced marriage. As Sieglinde swears her love in return, they tell one another more about their past lives. When the hero reveals that his father's real name was Walse, Sieglinde suddenly realizes that he is her long-lost twin brother, and their passion for one another is redoubled. Siegmund draws the gleaming sword from the great ash tree as the two lovers rejoice in this union of Walsung blood. They then rush out into the night.

ACT TWO, SCENE ONE

In a craggy mountainous wilderness, the mighty Wotan talks to his Valkyrie daughter Brunnhilde and tells her she must go into battle and give a just victory to his mortal son, Siegmund the Walsung, over Hunding. Joyfully, she obeys him and departs, just as Wotan's queen Fricka arrives upon a chariot drawn by two rams in the wake of a storm. Queen Fricka, who is also the goddess of marriage, insists that Hunding's sacred marriage rights must be defended and the Walsungs punished for adultery and incest. Wotan is forced against his will to enforce the law, for his power will leave him if he does not. Wotan swears an oath to command the death of Siegmund the Walsung. Queen Fricka victoriously rides off in her chariot.

SCENE TWO

Angered and saddened, Wotan now tells the Valkyrie Brunnhilde how Valhalla was bought with the ring, and how the ring was doubly cursed by Dwarfs and Rhinemaidens. To prevent disaster, Wotan went to the goddess Erda, with whom he conceived the nine Valkyries, who would gather in Valhalla a vast army of heroes to help defend the gods in their hour of need. Yet the fate of the world is dependent on Alberich's ring, for the Dwarf of Nibelheim still plots continually to seize the ring from the giant Fafner who broods over his golden treasure and guards it night and day. If the Nibelung eventually seizes the ring, the fate of the gods will be sealed. For by its power, Alberich will turn Wotan's heroic army against him and overthrow the gods. As Wotan is forbidden the ring, and only Alberich who has cursed love can command its power, the only hope for the gods is to be found in a mortal hero who is brave and strong enough to slay the giant and seize the ring on their behalf. To this end, the mortal hero Siegmund the Walsung was conceived and given a godly sword called Notung. But the curse of the ring is at work, for the laws of Fricka dictate that Wotan must order Brunnhilde to slay Siegmund.

SCENE THREE
The Valkyrie Brunnhilde sees Siegmund and Sieglinde approaching a rocky gorge and slips away. Siegmund comforts his sister-bride who hears the hunting-horn of Hunding in pursuit, and tells Siegmund to leave her and flee. Siegmund will not and swears to protect her with his sword, Notung, and tenderly comforts her until she falls into an exhausted sleep.

SCENE FOUR

Brunnhilde appears as if in a vision to Siegmund, leading her horse. Only warriors condemned to die can see the Valkyries, and Brunnhilde tells Siegmund that she will take him to Valhalla. Siegmund says he will not leave his sister-bride for the warriors' heaven. The Valkyrie tells him he has no choice, but Siegmund says he will make sure they are together in death. He takes out his sword with the intention of slaying both Sieglinde and himself. The Valkyrie stays his hand and swears she will violate the will of Wotan and give victory to Siegmund the Walsung.

SCENE FIVE

Siegmund leaves the sleeping Sieglinde and goes in search of Hunding. As the storm clouds flash and roar, the battle between the heroes commences upon a distant mountain ridge. Sieglinde wakes and is tormented by the sight of the conflict. Siegmund is protected by the Valkyrie's shield and Hunding is driven back. But just as Brunnhilde guides Siegmund's sword in what would certainly be a fatal blow, the storm clouds part and throb with fiery light. The fierce Wotan appears; he stands over Hunding and blocks Siegmund's stroke with the shaft of his spear. Siegmund's sword shatters and Hunding immediately plunges his own spear into the unarmed Siegmund's breast. Brunnhilde, seeing the hero lost, swiftly lifts Sieglinde onto her steed and rides away. Wotan remains sadly looking over the body of his mortal son Siegmund. Hunding pulls his spear from Siegmund's body, but stands too near the god. With a contemptuous wave of his hand, Wotan strikes Hunding dead; then vanishes in a flash of lightning.

ACT THREE, SCENE ONE

On the craggy heights of the Valkyrie Rock, the Valkyries arrive one by one with dead warriors across their saddles. The eight shield maidens gather to await Brunnhilde before they ride off to Valhalla. They are astonished when they see the rebel Valkyrie arrive with a living maiden across her saddle. They are filled with fear when they are told what has occurred. Sieglinde despairs and does not wish to live until Brunnhilde tells her that she is carrying Siegmund's child. For this she is thankful and determined to live. She takes the shards of the hero's sword from the Valkyrie, who also tells her that her son's name is to be Siegfried – victorious and free. Sieglinde is told to escape into the pine forest below the rock because Wotan avoids this place. In it lives the evil giant Fafner, who after long years of brooding over his treasure and his ring has become a great dragon. Sieglinde flees; while Brunnhilde bravely awaits Wotan's wrath.

SCENE TWO

Wotan appears before the Valkyries in a flash of fiery red light. In his fury he condemns Brunnhilde: she will lose all her supernatural powers and become a mortal man's wife. The other Valkyries are filled with horror at their sister's fate, and beg Wotan to have pity on her. Wotan silences them and drives them away by threatening them with the same fate.

SCENE THREE

Wotan and Brunnhilde remain alone on the rock. She claims that in defying his command she was actually doing his will and protecting his favourite mortal children, the Walsungs. But Wotan cannot take back his judgement. He tells her he will cast a spell of sleep on her. She will be left upon this rock for any mortal man to find, and when she is awakened she will be his prize. Sadly, Wotan tenderly kisses Brunnhilde's eyes and she falls into an enchanted sleep. Wotan lays her gently upon the ground, closes the visor of her helmet over her face and places her Valkyrie shield over her breast. Invoking Loge's fire, Wotan encircles the rock where the sleeping beauty lies with a wall of flame. Striking the rock as he departs, Wotan invokes a spell forbidding the rock to anyone who fears his spear.

'Siegfried'

ACT ONE, SCENE ONE

A large cave on the edge of a deep wood serves as a smithy for that ill-humoured Dwarf Mime, the brother of Alberich. Mime toils at the forge, complaining about his ungrateful foster son, Siegfried. The greedy Dwarf has no love for the powerful youth, but his plan is to get Siegfried to slay the dragon Fafner who lives nearby and so win the ring and treasure for Mime. The problem is that Mime doesn't have the skill to reforge the sword Notung, and all the swords he makes are not strong enough for the youth. Dressed in skins, the young Siegfried enters the smithy leading a huge bear on a rope, and jokingly has the bear chase the smith about the cave until he gives him his new sword. Once again, when Siegfried tries the blade, it breaks, and the youth scolds the Dwarf. Siegfried wonders at his dislike of this Dwarf who has nurtured him; something has always told him that Mime is evil. After threats from Siegfried, Mime finally tells the youth how his mother, Sieglinde, died in childbirth. Siegfried demands proof, so Mime shows him the fragments of the sword Notung. Siegfried rejoices and orders Mime to reforge the sword.

SCENE TWO

An ancient one-eyed man in a dark blue cloak enters the smithy. He is weary from his travels and uses a spear as a staff and wears a large broad-brimmed hat. He is called the Wanderer, but is actually Wotan in his earthly guise, and he asks the inhospitable Mime for shelter. The Dwarf tries to turn the traveller from his door, but the Wanderer challenges him to a contest of riddles, which will result in the loser giving up his head. The Wanderer easily answers Mime's three riddles – who lives under the earth (the Dwarfs or black-elves of Nibelheim), on it (the giants of Reisenheim), and above it (the gods or light-spirits of Valhalla). In return, Mime answers two of the Wanderer's riddles – name the family that Wotan loved best yet treated most harshly (the Walsungs), name the sword of the Walsungs (Notung). However, when the Wanderer asks him to name the one who can reforge Notung, Mime is beaten. The answer to the riddle is: only one who has never known fear can reforge the sword. To that same man, the Wanderer says, as he departs, he will leave the forfeit of Mime's head.

SCENE THREE

Siegfried returns for his sword and finds it not yet made. Mime now understands that Siegfried is the 'one who has never known fear' and desperately tries to teach him the 'meaning of fear'. This proves impossible, so Mime suggests that they go to visit Fafner the dragon, so the youth might learn about fear. Siegfried is keen to learn this new sensation, but decides that he must reforge his father's sword himself as Mime cannot. With sheer barbaric energy and demon strength, Siegfried succeeds where Mime has failed. As he works at the forge, the Dwarf cooks up a sleeping-potion for the youth. He believes that the youth will now slay Fafner the dragon, so the only way Mime may win the ring and save his life is to drug the youth and slay him while he sleeps. At last, the frenzy at the forge comes to a halt. Siegfried holds up the brilliant reforged blade of Notung. Then, with a single stroke, he splits the anvil in two.

ACT TWO, SCENE ONE

In the depths of a forest in the dark of night, Alberich the Nibelung watches Fafner's cave and broods over the ring. Wotan the Wanderer greets him in the dark. Alberich immediately recognizes him, but the god assures the Dwarf that he is not after the ring. He warns Alberich that his real rival is his brother

Mime. The young Siegfried knows nothing of the dragon's gold and the ring, and Wotan is banned from informing or helping him. Then the Wanderer calls out to wake the dragon. Both the Wanderer and Alberich offer to save Fafner's life in exchange for the ring, but the dragon finds this a ridiculous offer. He fears no one and goes back to sleep. Wotan laughs as he departs, telling Alberich he only woke the dragon to show the Dwarf how fate cannot be altered.

SCENE TWO

As day breaks, Siegfried and Mime climb to a knoll above the mouth of the dragon's cave. Mime leaves Siegfried alone and the youth blows his horn and wakes the dragon. Surprised, but not alarmed by Fafner's size, Siegfried jokes with the monster, and then asks him if he might teach him fear. The dragon grows impatient with the cocky youth and a titanic struggle ensues. The battle ends when Siegfried pierces the monster's heart. As Fafner dies, he warns the youth of the ring's curse. He also tells the hero that because of the ring, Siegfried will also soon die. Some of the dragon's blood drips on Siegfried's fingers and he puts them in his mouth. He finds, at once, that he can understand the language of birds. The Woodbird tells Siegfried about the dragon's gold, the magic Tarnhelm and the ring, which are to be found within the monster's cave.

SCENE THREE

The Dwarf brothers Alberich and Mime emerge from hiding. Seeing Fafner dead, they begin at once to argue over who will claim the treasure. Siegfried emerges from the dragon's cave with the ring on his hand and Tarnhelm tied to his belt. The Woodbird now warns him about Mime's plot. When Mime approaches and offers Siegfried a poisoned drink, the young hero cuts the Dwarf's head off, as Alberich laughs in the distance. Siegfried blocks the treasure-cave door with the body of the dragon. He then sets out on a new adventure when he is told by the Woodbird about a sleeping maiden who is to be found surrounded by a ring of fire on Valkyrie Rock.

ACT THREE, SCENE ONE

In a wild mountain pass, Wotan in his earthly guise as the Wanderer summons the prophetic goddess Erda and demands to learn the fate of the gods. When Erda will not give an answer, Wotan accepts that the doom of Valhalla is near. His remaining hope lies with the young hero Siegfried, who now holds the ring, and with Brunnhilde. He bequeaths the world to the Walsungs, and the race of mortal men.

SCENE TWO

In the midst of the god's reverie, Siegfried approaches. The Wanderer detains him and blocks his path. With a single stroke of the reforged Notung, Siegfried shatters Wotan's spear shaft. Thunder and lightning flash at his deed and the Wanderer vanishes. Siegfried goes on his way and is soon confronted by the wall of fire. He blows his horn and plunges fearlessly into the flames.

SCENE THREE

Siegfried emerges from the flames at Valkyrie Rock where he finds the sleeping, armoured warrior. However, when he removes the armour, he discovers the maiden Brunnhilde and is overwhelmed by her beauty. For the first time, he claims to understand what fear is, but he controls his trembling and wakens the sleeping beauty with a long kiss. Brunnhilde awakens to her lover. She soon realizes that by surrendering to Siegfried, she will lose her immortality, but she does so joyfully.

'The Twilight of the Gods'

PROLOGUE

Flames light up the Valkyrie Rock where the three fatal sisters, the Norns, sing of the ancient days of Wotan's great deeds, as they weave the golden cord of fate. They sing of the shattering of Wotan's spear of law and how this released Loge the god of fire, whose flames will soon consume Valhalla. They attempt to learn when the end will come, but the cord snaps. They understand that their own end has come, and they flee in terror to the caverns of Erda. As dawn comes, Siegfried and his bride Brunnhilde emerge from their cave. Although she is afraid that she may lose her lover, Brunnhilde knows how a warrior's heart yearns for adventure. She gives him her armour and her horse Grane to help in his quest. Siegfried swears his eternal love and gives Brunnhilde the ring as his constant pledge before he sets off into the Rhine valley.

ACT ONE, SCENE ONE

Gunther the king of the Gibichungs and his sister Gutrune sit enthroned in the vast hall of their castle on the Rhine. They are in council with their dark, brooding half-brother Hagen who advises them how they may increase the Gibichung dynasty's wealth and power. He tells them they both must soon marry: Gunther to the wise and beautiful Brunnhilde, and Gutrune to Siegfried the Dragonslayer who possesses the treasure of the Nibelung gold. This can only be achieved by guile. They agree that when the approaching hero comes, Gutrune will give him a magic potion that will make Siegfried forget Brunnhilde and fall in love with Gutrune.

SCENE TWO

Siegfried's horn sounds from a river boat as he approaches the castle. Hagen and Gunther welcome him with friendship and honour, and Gutrune brings to him a horned cup with the fatal magic potion. Though he toasts them in the name of his lover Brunnhilde, the moment after the drink leaves his lips he opens his eyes and heart to Gutrune. He swears his undying love for her and asks for her hand in marriage. Gunther agrees on the condition that Siegfried win for him the fair Brunnhilde, whose name now means nothing to the drugged Siegfried. Hagen advises Siegfried that they may achieve their aim with the Tarnhelm, by whose magic he may change his shape to that of Gunther. Gunther and Siegfried swear blood oaths of brotherhood and ride off on their adventure.

SCENE THREE

On the Valkyrie Rock, Brunnhilde calls out a greeting of welcome to a sister Valkyrie. But the Valkyrie brings news of disorder and degeneration in Valhalla since Wotan's spear was shattered. Wotan has no authority to rule or act, and nothing will lift the curse of the ring except its return to its rightful guardians. But Brunnhilde angrily refuses to return the ring to the Rhinemaidens, and drives her sister away. The ring is the token of Siegfried's love and nothing will make her part with it. After the Valkyrie's departure, however, a strange man penetrates the flames of the wall of fire. It is Siegfried wearing Tarnhelm which has changed him to Gunther's form. As Gunther the Gibichung, he claims Brunnhilde as his bride because he has passed the test of the ring of fire. After he seizes the ring from her hand, Brunnhilde has no power to resist him. He carries her off into the cave as his bride, but resolves to lay his sword between them as they sleep, so as not to dishonour his blood-brother.

ACT TWO, SCENE ONE

In front of the Gibichung hall on the bank of the Rhine, Hagen, armed with spear and shield, is leaning against a doorpost, asleep. It is dark, but in the moonlight Alberich the Nibelung appears to Hagen in a dream. It is revealed that Hagen is the son of Alberich from a loveless union with Gunther's mother. Alberich makes his unhappy son swear that he will win back the Nibelung's ring.

SCENE TWO

As dawn breaks, Hagen awakens and Siegfried joyfully returns and greets him and Gutrune with the news that he has won Brunnhilde for King Gunther. He tells how he remained faithful that night, and then how on the journey back Gunther came and took Siegfried's place, while Siegfried used the power of Tarnhelm to reach the Gibichung castle ahead of them.

SCENE THREE

Hagen has summoned all the vassals of the kingdom to welcome King Gunther and his new queen. They offer up sacrifices to the altars of the gods and swear to uphold the new queen's honour.

SCENE FOUR

When Gunther arrives to present his new bride, Brunnhilde sees Siegfried with the ring upon his hand. She realizes at once that Gunther treacherously won her by deception. Siegfried the Walsung, she tells all, is her true husband. Siegfried swears upon the point of Hagen's spear that he has never known this woman as a bride. Brunnhilde is inflamed with a sense of betrayal and swears that his oath is false and that his sword hung on the wall, not between them. Siegfried denies the charge and leaves with Gutrune, although the vassals clearly believe Brunnhilde's story.

SCENE FIVE

Brunnhilde is devastated and bent on vengeance for her betrayal. She turns to Hagen, and tells him that Siegfried is protected from all weapons by a magic spell she wove. There is one way Siegfried may be slain, however; because she knew he would never flee from battle, the spell does not protect his back. So if Hagen drives his spear blade into Siegfried's back, he will die. Brunnhilde's taunts, and Hagen's promises of wealth and power, eventually persuade Gunther to join in the conspiracy to murder, as Siegfried's wedding procession passes by.

ACT THREE, SCENE ONE

In a woodland on the banks of the Rhine, the three Rhinemaidens lament their lost gold. When Siegfried, who is out hunting, appears, they plead that he give back the ring, but he refuses. They warn him that if he does not return it to the Rhine, he will be slain this day.

SCENE TWO

When the rest of the hunting party arrives, Hagen and Gunther urge Siegfried to entertain them with tales of his childhood with Mime and his slaying of Fafner the Dragon. Finally, after giving him a drink to revive his memory, Hagen asks him to tell of the wooing of Brunnhilde. With a pretence of moral outrage, Hagen drives his spear into the hero's back. Calling out his love for Brunnhilde with his last breath, Siegfried dies.

SCENE THREE

In front of the Gibichung hall in the moonlight, Gutrune is anxiously waiting as an evil dream wakes her in the night. Hagen comes to tell her that Siegfried has been killed by a wild boar. However, when his body is carried in, Gutrune will have none of it. She accuses Gunther of murder, but Gunther denies it and curses Hagen. Hagen defiantly admits the murder, but says it was justice. Then he claims the golden ring for himself. When Gunther disputes his right, Hagen slays him. Yet when he is about to seize the ring, the dead Siegfried's hand rises threateningly against him. Hagen falls back in fear, as Brunnhilde commands all to stand back from the hero. She orders a funeral pyre to be made for Siegfried. She then takes the ring and places it on her own finger. Then Brunnhilde torches the pyre, calls on the Rhine-maidens to retrieve the gold from her ashes, then rides Grane into the flames. The Rhine overflows its banks as the Gibichung hall is also consumed in the flames. The Rhinemaidens rise with the river. They joyfully seize the ring, and vengefully drag the damned Hagen down to a watery grave. The flood subsides to leave only the burnt ruin of the hall, but in the distance, in the heavens, Valhalla can be seen catching alight, and is finally entirely consumed by flames.

CHAPTER SIXTEEN

TOLKIEN'S RING

In *Tolkien's Ring*, we have followed the symbol of the ring and the tradition of the ring quest through the millennia. In so doing, we have seen how Tolkien drew on the myth, history and literature of a score of cultures in the creation of his multi-layered epic tale *The Lord of the Rings*. Without rejecting its heritage, however, Tolkien radically transformed the ring quest and made it into something fresh and relevant to the twentieth century.

Each age has its use for the ring quest, and special circumstances or 'accidents of history' in the twentieth century have made Tolkien's version of that quest not only relevant and meaningful but, to some degree, prophetic.

That is not to say that *The Lord of the Rings* is an allegory of our time. Tolkien rightly rejected the allegorical view as too narrow for his tale. He especially abhorred questions of the 'Are Orcs Nazis or Communists?' kind. Tolkien's purpose was both more specific and more universal.

He once wrote: 'I think that many confuse "applicability" with "allegory", but the one resides in the freedom of the reader, and the other in the purposed domination of the author.' In *The Lord of the Rings*, Tolkien gives us an adventure in the form of a ring quest with a simple human moral truth at its centre. However, the nature of that adventure and that moral position were undeniably 'applicable' to the most dramatic conflicts of the twentieth century.

Although Tolkien did not intend to mimic the events of his time, he did acknowledge when he began writing *The Lord of the Rings* in 1937 that something of the impending conflict with Nazi Germany was discernible in the dark atmosphere of its composition. Furthermore, as the bulk of the book was written through the dark years of World War II, there were aspects of the real war that were inevitably comparable to his 'War of the Ring'.

It is interesting to note Tolkien's own comments on this in his wartime letters to his son, Christopher, who was stationed with the British forces in South Africa. He sent chapters in serial form to Christopher as he wrote them, along with personal letters with constant references to Hobbits, Orcs and Rings – as similes for individuals and issues relating to actual events in the conflict with Germany.

'Well, there you are: a hobbit among the Urukhai,' Tolkien wrote. 'Keep your hobbitry in heart and think that all stories feel like that when you are in them.' However, this did not mean that real events in the war shaped Tolkien's invented war. His 'War of the Ring' was about ideals, not political realities. It essentially revolved around a human moral crisis which he perceived in the real war, but not just in the enemy.

In one letter to Christopher, Tolkien wrote: 'We are attempting to conquer Sauron with the Ring. And we shall (it seems) succeed. But the penalty is, as you will know, to breed new Saurons, and slowly turn Men and Elves into Orcs. Not that in real life things are as clear-cut as in a story, and we started out with a great many Orcs on our side...'

Clearly, Tolkien's war had its own direction to follow which had no parallels in the war with Germany. This is not to say that Tolkien was neutral in his view of Hitler and Nazi Germany – far from it.

In 1941, he wrote to another son, Michael, who was at the time an officer cadet at the Royal Military Academy at Sandhurst.

I have spent most of my life, since I was your age, studying Germanic matters (in the general sense that includes England and Scandinavia). There is a great deal more force (and truth) than ignorant people imagine in the 'Germanic' ideal ... Anyway, I have in this War a burning private grudge – which would probably make me a better soldier at 49 than I was at 22: against that ruddy little ignoramus Adolf Hitler. Ruining, perverting, misapplying, and making for ever accursed that noble northern spirit, a supreme contribution to Europe, which I have ever loved, and tried to present in its true light. Nowhere, incidentally, was it nobler than in England, nor more early sanctified ...

Indeed, one might even perceive that this 'grudge' against Hitler might have had something to do with Tolkien's ambitions in writing a new version of the ring quest. In the nineteenth century, Richard Wagner recognized the absolute centrality of the ring quest in the vast mythological themes of European and especially Germanic peoples. He consciously seized upon the ring as a symbol of the German identity, heritage and state. In the twentieth century, the music of Wagner's *The Ring of the Nibelung* became so closely allied with the Nazi Party and the rise of the Third Reich that they became synonymous in the popular mind. During World War II, the grand themes and traditions of the ring quest were usurped (or, as Tolkien saw it, ruined, perverted and misapplied) by the German state with which Tolkien's nation was at war.

On one level, *The Lord of the Rings* is certainly an attempt by Tolkien to reclaim the ring as a symbol of 'that noble northern spirit' which had fallen into such disrepute in Germany. With some justification, Tolkien blamed Wagner and his heirs for the dimming of the 'true light'. Although Wagner's genius was indisputable, his politics were repugnant. The great musician's family and heirs were not innocent dupes of the Nazi Party. Wagner's ideological stance may to some degree be evaluated by the fact that he chose to dedicate his collected works to Arthur de Gobineau, the father of Aryan racialist theory – a theory that Tolkien correctly rejected as being as intellectually ridiculous as it was morally repellent.

To Tolkien's credit, he saw from the beginning the nature of the Nazi obsession with Wagner's Ring Cycle. What appealed to the Nazis in the ring quest was an idealization of the pursuit of power for its own sake. Tolkien appreciated the ring quest tradition on many levels, but having already lived through one world war, he understood the nature of the curse of the 'ring of power' as well as any man could. He believed that even for the good man the pursuit of power was in itself an evil that would enslave the human spirit and soul. And, in the Third Reich, there were not many 'good men' to start with.

There can be little doubt that part of Tolkien's deeply felt motivation in writing *The Lord of the Rings* was a desire to set the record straight by reclaiming the ring quest tradition, and presenting the 'noble northern spirit' of Europe in its 'true light'. Just as Tolkien chose on minor points to 'challenge' Shakespeare's use of myth and history in *Macbeth*, so on a much grander scale he 'challenged' Wagner's use of myth and history in his Ring Cycle operas by writing *The Lord of the Rings*.

Tolkien understood the deep moral crisis at the centre of the ring quest as Wagner perceived it. He saw the devastation that the Iron Age mentality of the ring quest had wreaked in the world, and chose to reshape the ring quest fundamentally for the twentieth century. He did this by turning the quest on its head. The ring of power was 'unmade' by reversing the spell. The hero of the quest does not seize the ring but destroys it by dropping it into the inferno where it was made.

In 1937, Tolkien began to forge his 'One Ring' imaginatively as a symbol for an absolute power that morally and physically contaminated all who touched it. He could not even have guessed how soon history would catch up with his dark vision and make his tale appear almost prophetic. He certainly could not have imagined how the scientists of the real world would soon create something that was every bit as powerful, evil and contaminating as the 'One Ring' of Sauron the Dark Lord.

Although *The Lord of the Rings* was largely written during the war years, it was not published until 1954, and, by this time, the atomic bomb had seized the popular imagination. The public was less likely to equate Sauron with Hitler than the One Ring with the Bomb. It was difficult for many to believe that the idea of the One Ring was not inspired by the Bomb. Surely, some suggested, no place could look more like a nuclear testing ground than the ash-laden land of Mordor?

There is no doubt that Tolkien was very much against the atomic bomb. On 9 August 1945, he wrote to Christopher: 'The news today about "Atomic bombs" is so horrifying one is stunned. The utter folly of these lunatic physicists to consent to do such work for war purposes: calmly plotting the destruction of the world!'

Still, Tolkien was at pains to point out that the One Ring was fully formed long before he had any idea of the activities of atomic scientists. In a letter written in 1956, he found it necessary to state: 'Of course my story is not an allegory of Atomic power, but of Power (exerted for Domination).' However, he had to acknowledge that in a larger sense the message or moral of his novel certainly did not exclude atomic power.

Indeed, Tolkien's views on nuclear weapons would not have been at all out of place at any CND or Ban the Bomb meeting or protest march.

Nuclear physics can be used for that purpose [bombs]. But they need not be. They need not be used at all. If there is any contemporary reference in my story at all it is to what seems to me the most widespread assumption of our time: that if a thing can be done, it must be done. This seems to me wholly false. The greatest examples of the action of the spirit and of reason are in abnegation. When you say Atomic power is 'here to stay' you remind me that

Chesterton said that whenever he heard that, he knew that whatever it referred to would soon be replaced, and thought pitifully
shabby and old-fashioned. So-called 'atomic' power is rather bigger
than anything he was thinking of (I have heard it of trams, gas-
light, steam-trains). But it surely is clear that there will have to be
some 'abnegation' in its use, a deliberate refusal to do some of the
things it is possible to do with it, or nothing will stay!

Even retrospectively, however, it still seems very unlikely that such a self-
confessed 'old fogey' of an Anglo-Saxon professor, writing about a remote
imaginary world filled with an impossibly obscure invented mythology, could
suddenly find a huge American campus cult following in the midst of the
radical, politically charged 1960s. Tolkien was nobody's idea of a radical campus
professor, so what was it in his writing that was suddenly so relevant to the lives
and politics of the youth culture of the 1960s, catapulting him into the category
of one of the most popular authors of the century?

The answer was that Tolkien's approach to the ancient grand theme of the
ring quest was as unconventional and inventive as his unlikely heroes, the
Hobbits. In fact, *The Lord of the Rings* proved to be the perfect student counter-
culture book. It was full of action and adventure, but it appeared ultimately to
hold an anti-establishment, pacifist message. Frodo Baggins might not have
been exactly a Hobbit Gandhi, but he did reject the temptations of worldly
power to an almost saintly degree. The student anti-war and ban the bomb
movements of the sixties found an empathetic anti-hero in the Hobbit's humble
values, as did the back-to-the-land hippy drop-out culture. Tolkien could not
have touched more bases with the youth culture of the sixties if he had commis-
sioned a market survey.

If Tolkien was ambiguous about the 'meaning' of his tale, there is no doubt
that the parallels between the One Ring and the Bomb were not missed by
activists in the late sixties and early seventies. One need only read Robert
Hunter's *The Greenpeace Chronicles* to see how closely allied the counter-culture
was with Tolkien's world. Greenpeace came into being in 1969 in Vancouver,
Canada, as an ecological guerrilla organization that attempted to stop American
nuclear testing on Amchitka Island in Alaska. To this end, it chartered its first
ship and attempted to prevent the bomb from being exploded by sailing into
the test area.

Writing about this maiden Greenpeace voyage, Hunter tells how they had
arrived at a point where even the stout hearts of his shipmates saw their task as
rather comically hopeless. 'There was something superbly comical about it: here

we were, eight green-clad amateur seamen, on our way to confront the deadliest fire of the age, like Hobbits bearing the ring towards the volcano of Mordor.'

It was a comparison that carried them a long way. Like exhausted Hobbits they persevered. If Hobbits could overcome the forces of Sauron, why couldn't a ragtag band of hippies overthrow the US military-industrial complex? At one point the valves and pistons of the old engine of their rather battered vessel required such coaxing and constant care on their long voyage along the north Pacific coast that the activists dubbed themselves the 'Fellowship of the Piston Rings'.

In Tolkien's tale, when the One Ring is finally destroyed, the subsequent volcanic eruption closely resembles a nuclear explosion – but an explosion that destroys only the evil forces of the Ring Lord. One might also see in that explosive 'unmaking' of the One Ring the reversal of the traditional ring quest in a moral sense as well. That Iron Age mentality of 'might equals right' which made the ring quest for power so important ends with the nuclear age – when possession of such power entails only mutual destruction.

It was Albert Einstein who warned the world: 'The unleashing power of the atom has changed everything except our way of thinking ... we need an essentially new way of thinking if mankind is to survive.'

Tolkien's reversal of the ring quest demonstrates this 'new way of thinking'. Its version of the quest represents a desire to change power structures. Tolkien saw the results of the pursuit of pure power in two wars, and rejected it. In his private mythic world he understood a human truth that modern technology has brought home to mankind with a terrible vengeance in the form of the nuclear bomb. If ever there was a manifestation of the ultimate power of the One Ring, the Bomb was it. The 'Cold War' was the result of the grudging admission that power of the kind represented by nuclear weapons was ultimately self-destructive.

Tolkien also displayed this 'new way of thinking' in his inspired choice of heroes. One must not forget the importance of his Hobbits; it would do no good to change the nature of the quest without changing the nature of the hero. Not only did Tolkien turn the ring quest on its head; he also reversed many of the characteristics usually expected of the quest hero. He wrote:

> The Hobbits are, of course, really meant to be a branch of the specifically human race (not Elves or Dwarves) ... They are entirely without non-human powers, but are represented as being more in touch with 'nature', and abnormally, for humans, free from ambi-

tion or greed of wealth. They are made small partly to exhibit the pettiness of man, plain unimaginative parochial man ... and mostly to show up, in creatures of very small physical power, the amazing and unexpected heroism of ordinary men 'at a pinch'.

Ultimately, the greatest strength of Tolkien's Hobbits in their epic struggle against all odds is their basic human decency. It is their essential humanity, their simple but pure human spirits, that allowed them to triumph in the end. And it is this human element, combined with the grandeur and pomp of a magnificently conceived mythic world, that has been the key to Tolkien's continued popularity.

Characteristically, however, Frodo Baggins, the Hobbit, actually fails to live up to the classic 'hero' image at the time of the ultimate test. At the last moment, on the edge of the Crack of Doom, the Hobbit's resolve fails and he refuses to destroy the One Ring. Virtuous though Frodo is, it is not the strength of his will that allows the One Ring to be destroyed and Middle-earth to be saved. It is Frodo's unprovoked and almost foolish charity towards an undeserving enemy. Out of a sense of mercy, the Hobbit allows the treacherous Gollum to live. Reason should tell Frodo that Gollum will betray him again, but the Hobbit chooses to obey his heart. In the end, the One Ring is destroyed exactly because Frodo takes pity on his enemy, and Gollum survives long enough to betray him again. On the edge of the Crack of Doom, Gollum wrestles with the Hobbit. Finally, he overcomes the weakened Frodo. He viciously bites off the Hobbit's ring finger. Then, seizing the One Ring, Gollum topples backward into the fiery abyss. The One Ring is destroyed.

In Frodo the Hobbit, Tolkien found a twentieth-century Everyman who has, and will continue to have, universal appeal to people of any time and any place. In Tolkien's *The Lord of the Rings* the Hobbit teaches us that 'attempting to conquer Sauron with the ring' is no longer the goal of the quest. In the end, it is not the power of the mind nor the strength of the body but the instincts of the human heart that save the world. It is the simple human capacity for mercy that finally allows evil to be overthrown.